Writing:
Steps to Success
Level 5 to 6 +

Kevin Eames Karyn Taylor David Trelawny-Ross
Consultant: Debra Myhill

Hodder & Stoughton

A MEMBER OF THE HODDER HEADLINE GROUP

Acknowledgements:

The authors and publishers would like to thank the following for their kind permission to reproduce copyright material:

Copyright Text:
ppix–x two extracts from English Text Mark Scheme for Paper 1, 2000 © Qualifications and Curriculum Authority; pp7, 13–14, 19, 23 all extracts from *Coram Boy* by Jamila Gavin; pp10, 20 all extracts from *After the First Death* by Robert Cormier (Victor Gollanz 1979) © Robert Cormier, 1979; pp34–35 an extract from *The Trials of Life* by David Attenborough, from *Life Trilogy*; p38 an extract from *To the Ends of the Earth* by Ranulph Fiennes, published by Sinclair-Stevenson. Used by permission of The Random House Group Limited; pp41–42 an extract from *Following Seas, Sailing the Globe Sounding a Life* by Beth A. Leonard © 1996 Beth A. Leonard; pp55, 58, 61, 62 all extracts from a Médicins Sans Frontiéres leaflet, reproduced by permission of Médicins Sons Frontiéres; pp73–74, 79 all examples of a student's work, reproduced by permission of Sian Ahmed.

Copyright Photographs:
p39 Eugenie Glacier © Geray Sweeney/Corbis; p42 Roger Ressmeyer © Corbis; p53 and 64 three female doctors and patient, Kosovo © Roger Job; p55 © Grant Leaity p61 MSF's doctor in a refugee camp – Benguela Nutrition Center MSF, Angola © Gilles Sauisser/Still Pictures.

Copyright Artworks:
Pat Murray: ppxii–xiv, 1, 3, 6, 8, 9–12, 14, 15, 17, 21-22, 27, 30, 33, 36, 37, 43, 44, 47, 52, 60, 67, 70, 79, 82, 83.
Dave Hancock: pp2, 29, 48, 69.

Every effort has been made to trace copyright holders of material reproduced in this book. Any rights not acknowledged will be acknowledged in subsequent printings if notice is given to the publisher.

Orders: please contact Bookpoint Ltd, 130 Milton Park, Abingdon, Oxon OX14 4SB. Telephone: (44) 01235 827720, Fax: (44) 01235 400454. Lines are open from 9.00–6.00, Monday to Saturday, with a 24 hour message answering service. You can also order through our website www.hodderheadline.co.uk

British Library Cataloguing in Publication Data
A catalogue record for this title is available from The British Library

ISBN 0 340 84520 1

First published 2002
Impression number   10 9 8 7 6 5 4 3 2
Year   2008 2007 2006 2005 2004 2003

Copyright © 2002 Kevin Eames, Karyn Taylor, David Trelawny-Ross

Cover photo from Michael Stones.
Typeset by Fakenham Photosetting Limited, Fakenham, Norfolk.
Printed in Great Britain for Hodder & Stoughton Educational, a division of Hodder Headline, 338 Euston Road, London NW1 3BH by J.W. Arrowsmith Ltd., Bristol.

CONTENTS

Teachers' Introduction

This book:

1   **places continual emphasis on letting students know exactly what they need to do for success at a particular level**

2   **breaks down success into bite-size achievable targets, particularly relevant to the learning needs of boys**

3   **covers all the different text-types in the Key Stage 3 Literacy Framework**

4   **focuses on sentence level work, to improve students' control over sentence construction**

5   **draws on approaches to writing embodied in the Key Stage 3 Literacy Strategy and the Progress Units**

6   **is designed to be used either with specific ability groups, in a mixed ability class, or with different year groups**

7   **aims to keep the writing process real.**

This book:

1   **places continual emphasis on letting students know exactly what they need to do for success at a particular level**

Writing: Steps to Success is intended to help students who are currently working at a specified level to improve their writing skills so that they are able, independently, to write at a higher level. It aims to do this by giving students a detailed awareness of what writing at their target level looks like, and by making sure they are clear about what exactly they need to do to write at that level. Each book begins with a detailed comparison of two pieces of writing by students, one at the lower and the other at the upper level. Accompanying the texts is a thorough commentary, making very explicit the distinct features that differentiate the two texts from each other. The aim is to help students to be very clear about the skills they need to develop to progress from the lower to the upper level, or to consolidate and broaden their achievement if they are already beginning to write at the upper level.

2 **breaks down success into bite-size achievable targets, particularly relevant to the learning needs of boys**

Each book breaks down the skills needed to write at each level into a set of small achievable targets. As is now generally recognised, boys in particular benefit from having it made very clear to them what exactly they need to do, in small steps, to make progress. Each unit, therefore, breaks down the task of writing a particular text-type into the separate skills, mastery of which is needed to write at the level the student is working towards. In addition, each book builds on the skills learnt in the previous book. There is, therefore, a clear progression in the skills being taught so that students grow in the confidence and complexity with which they are able to demonstrate the skills essential for successful writing. Each book also focuses on the objectives of one year: **Writing: Steps to Success Level 5 to 6^{+}** uses the Framework Objectives for Year 9 as a starting point. Together, therefore, the three books provide a chronological progression as well as a skills progression.

3 **covers all the different text-types in the Key Stage 3 Literacy Framework**

In organisation, **Writing: Steps to Success** is very simple and clear. At the beginning of each book is a Students' Introduction with examples of students' work at the lower and upper levels relevant to that book. Through a discussion of these, students are able to form a clear picture of the differences in writing at the two levels, and to begin establishing their own targets for the skills they need to improve their own writing. Each book then has four units, each unit guiding students through the production of a piece of writing in each of the text-type triplets described in the Key Stage 3 Literacy Framework and National Curriculum 2000 document. In doing this, it ensures that the main text and sentence level objectives in the Literacy Framework for Key Stage 3 Writing are covered.

4 **focuses on sentence level work, to improve students' control over sentence construction**

The books do not aim to cover all the text and sentence level objectives. However, there is a continual emphasis on improving students' ability to control and extend their sentences, this being essential to success at a higher level. As a result, within each unit, there is a significant emphasis on developing their sentence level skills and all the sentence level objectives that are important in moving students from one level to the next are covered.

5   draws on approaches to writing embodied in the Key Stage 3 Literacy Strategy and the Progress Units

Writing: Steps to Success draws on the established best practice of English teachers and on the model of teaching writing provided by the Key Stage 3 Literacy Strategy. All units follow a similar structure. Each unit begins with a description of the particular type of writing. It then establishes the features of the type of writing, in particular, the features of that type of writing at the level relevant to that book. Students have to assess their own skills in this type of writing and, through self-assessment, set themselves the targets that they need to reach to improve their writing from one level to the next. The description and self-assessment are followed by a series of activities which guide students through the planning and writing of a text. In each unit there is a set of activities clearly focused on developing the discrete skills necessary to write successfully at the target level, with emphasis on how to improve the complexity of their sentence writing. Throughout, students are encouraged to check their work to ensure that they have met the specific criteria for success. Each unit ends with further opportunities for students to write texts of that type. These opportunities are intended to move students from being dependent on the scaffolding provided by the book and their teacher, to being independent writers, with the requisite skills for successful writing internalised.

6   is designed to be used either with specific ability groups, in a mixed ability class, or with different year groups

The three books are not designed to be a replacement to existing schemes of work, but as a supplementary resource. If, as part of a scheme of work, a teacher wants to develop his or her students' expertise in a particular type of writing, the books provide detailed advice on how students can achieve such expertise. The books are not intended in any way to replace the teacher. Even though the activities are written with the students as the audience and are intended to help students develop skills independently, the role of the teacher is seen as essential, in leading students through the process, and in providing opportunities to reinforce or clarify where necessary. The expertise of the teacher, therefore, is indispensable in deciding on pace, timing, groupings, and so on. It is assumed, also, that teachers will need to remind pupils of terminology, for example, clause, connective. Even at Level 3 to 4⁺, a growing familiarity with linguistic terms, and confidence in using and applying them, will enhance the capacity of students to develop independence as writers. It is not assumed, though, that the simple recitation of terms is of value; at all times, the identification of linguistic features should be related to their effect on meaning.

Obviously, each book is particularly focused on the needs of students at one level who need to move up to the next. However, the skills taught and practised in each unit will be relevant to a far wider group than just students at the lower level of each book. A student who has attained a certain level according to their test results may well still need to learn further key skills, in order to work confidently and consistently at the level identified. The activities, therefore, provide opportunities for students to achieve a more thorough grasp of the skills necessary for success at a particular level, or for them to consolidate skills only tentatively grasped. As a result, the books do not need to be restricted to a group where all students are at the target level.

There are probably three main ways in which the books can be used. In a mixed ability class, all three books could be used concurrently, with groups of different attainment using the book relevant to their level. In a setted environment, the book most relevant to the attainment of that group could be used. Alternatively, since each book uses the Framework Objectives for one of the years at Key Stage 3 as a starting point, a different book could be used with each of Years 7 to 9.

7 aims to keep the writing process real

While the books embody the belief that students need to be very clear about the criteria necessary for success, the authors are aware that writing should not become simply a menu of skills to be ticked off. Equally, with the demands of writing in such a wide range of types, there is the danger that the process is reduced simply to the speedy production of very short pieces of writing displaying a narrow set of skills. Aware of these dangers, the authors want to emphasise that each unit provides opportunities to produce a substantial text, with the process marked by the familiar stages of the writing journey, and its concern to shape meaning clearly and appropriately. Accordingly, students will plan, draft, check, redraft, and reflect, as they seek to produce writing that is lively and imaginative, committed and engaging.

Ultimately, the aim is to let students in on the secret of how to write effectively in a variety of text-types, and in so doing to give them more power and more control over what they do, thus guiding them on the road to being real and successful writers.

Students' Introduction

How can I improve my writing from Level 5 to Level 6⁺?

To continue to improve your writing you need to know the features of writing at different levels. What are the features of writing at Level 5? How can you improve your work to reach Level 6⁺? These pages will help you to focus on some of the differences in attainment and will give you an idea of what features to target in your own work.

Read the two pieces below, and on the next page. The writers had to carry out this task under test conditions:

Write a description of a place which is unwelcoming or isolated.

In your writing, try to use a variety of sentence structures and interesting vocabulary to create a sense of place for the reader.
You could write about a place which is:
- *real or made up*
- *busy or deserted.*

Text One

The trees made rustling sound like a ghost whos moaning. The shadows looked like people watching you. The building so derelict that no-one could have ever lived there. It was scary and the wind sounded like moaning ghosts.

No-one ever went there. It was isolated, on its own in the middle of the wood. It had boarded up windows and the floorboards squeaked when you walked on them. It was dirty and dusty. It smelt of smoke and rust. It had no roof, this was because it had been on fire a couple of times. The ashes were still there, an inch thick on the floor, but were very compressed.

People say that people had been murdered here, but I think it is a rumour. Other people think it is haunted, but I don't know and I don't really care.

My friends go to the 'barn' every week, but Im disallowed. I'm not bothered because it scares me and I don't like it.

The woods make it worse. The darkness and the wind rustling through the trees. The sticks and twigs crunch on the ground when you walk. The noise echoes and you think someone is following. That scares me a lot.

Text Two

The Reston Mansion had been deserted for nearly a whole decade now. Most of the local neighbours were terrified to go anywhere near the front entrance. Because thats where the whole tragic event started.

Many rumours and warnings had been spread around the medium size village of Whipville. All parents forbade their children to go there.

The exterior of the mansion was a dark, dusty grey like the colour of ashes. Most of the windows had either cracks or large gaps where children threw rocks. The door was large and thick with worm holes and cobwebs. The previously polished brass knocker was now a worn down rusty metal block hanging off the door. The front garden was full of overgrown weeds and stinging nettles where small black flies liked to hover. Because of the viney weeds, the terracotta path could barely be visible.

Inside, the once grand staircase is now home to an inch of dust. Once the family fled, the dust began to invade the mansion and form a misty blanket of all the furniture. You could almost imagine the whole family relaxing in front of the beautifully decorated fireplace. Now, with all the elegant vases and figurines, the warmth and homeliness of the mansion has been overcome by the cold and neglect.

In the kitchen, the radio is still plugged in. This was the maid's headquarters, now it is the headquarters of emptiness.

Upstairs in one of the bedrooms, the bed is neatly made and the hair brush on the table still holds the hairs of the previous user. Here, you can see the only part of the house which has been protected from the dust – the wardrobe. It contains a woman's old dresses and slippers. The mirror is intact however the wardrobe has become damp from the weather. Now the only thing that can be restored is the building. The neglect of the property has resulted in the destruction of all the fragile properties and the thimble collection which was once the lady of the House's pride and joy.

The nursery upstairs is still scattered with all the child's toys and baby books. The tiny bed, where the parents sang lullabies to the baby every night, is still made up untouched by a human hand since the sudden departure of the family.

Back downstairs, a pile of newspapers can barely be recognised on the coffee table. A china mug on the floor near the red leather armchair holds the remains of a cup of tea or coffee which the father was in the middle of drinking during reading the Sunday paper.

Because it is a listed building, nobody are allowed to demolish or restore the building. The Reston Mansion is now in the hands of nature which is the only thing that cares about it. All the memories fade away …

Discussion of the texts

These pieces were both written under test conditions. There are, of course, many things that the writers would have redrafted if they had had the time during their tests. However, Text One was graded as Level 5 and Text Two was graded at Level 7. Although the second text does a lot more than you will need to do to get a Level 6, the features of the writing in Text Two are the same as the ones you will be learning about to get a Level 6.

Think about the task that was set. Discuss with your partner what the writers were being asked to do.

- Think about the **purpose** of the writing. This task asked for a **description**. An effective piece of descriptive writing makes it easy for the reader to imagine the place being described. They should be able to feel what the place is like. Do you feel that the writers have described their chosen places effectively?
- A descriptive piece of writing should also **grab and hold your attention** and make you want to read on. Do either of these pieces do that? What do the writers do to make their writing interesting or gripping?
- The writers were asked to write about a place that is unwelcoming or isolated. Have both writers chosen an **appropriate place** for their piece of writing? Have they included details that make their place seem unwelcoming or isolated? Has either writer chosen a style that fits a piece of writing about an unwelcoming or isolated place?
- Have the writers used an adventurous choice of **vocabulary** effectively, to make their writing more interesting?

Now look in more detail at sentence level.

- Are these writers accurate in their use of **full stops** and **capital letters** almost all the time?
- What about **commas**? Do they use commas to mark off **phrases** and **clauses** in a sentence? All the time, or some of the time? Do they use both **single commas** and **sets of commas**, where appropriate?
- When they write sentences with more than one clause, do they vary their sentences with **subordinate clauses, co-ordinate clauses**, or a **mixture** of the two?
- Have they controlled the **length of sentences** for effect? For example, do they use a short sentence suddenly to make the reader stop and to build up tension?
- Do they vary the way in which they **structure** their sentences, so that they do not always start sentences with a noun, pronoun or noun phrase?
- Has either writer used a **passive voice**? If so, what effect does it have on the sentence? Does it help emphasise the main topic of the sentence? Does it give a variety to the sentences that makes the text more interesting?
- Have both writers written in **paragraphs**? Has either used paragraphs to give the piece a structure or flow? What different reasons can you see for writers starting a new paragraph? Do they start a new paragraph to show a change in time or a change in subject?
- Do the writers link sentences and paragraphs with a wide range of **connectives** to signpost the reader through the text?

What did you spot?

Now compare what you and your partner noticed with the points below. Look first at whole-text level:

- In these examples, the writers were asked for a **description** of a place that is unwelcoming or isolated. Both writers have written a description of a deserted house. Both have been successful in making the house seem isolated by telling the reader that no-one visits the house. Both have made the house seem unwelcoming by telling the reader that people are too scared to go there or that children are forbidden from visiting the house. They also have included **details** that make the house sound unwelcoming: the writer of Text One describes shadows and boarded up windows, while the writer of Text Two describes the broken windows and an overgrown garden. In both texts, these details make it easy for us to picture the house.

- Both writers are successful at **grabbing our attention**. The writer of Text One made the place sound spooky by mentioning trees sounding like ghosts and, later on, by telling us of the rumours that surround the house. We want to know what lies behind the rumours. The writer of Text Two grabs our attention more successfully than the writer of Text One, by being more focused and precise in the information we are given: the house has been deserted for *nearly a whole decade* (not just a long time); *most of the local neighbours* (not just people) are terrified to go there. As with Text One, we want to know why it is deserted, and why locals won't go there.

- Both writers have chosen a **place** and selected the kind of **description** that is appropriate to this kind of writing. Text One mentions *the trees making a rustling sound like a ghost, boarded up windows* and *floorboards that squeaked when you walked on them*. All these are the kinds of details you would expect in a description that would not be out of place in a horror or ghost story. The same is true of Text Two, but, again, Text Two is more successful. The writer uses much more detail in the description; compare the simple description of *boarded up windows* in Text One with this sentence: *Most of the windows had either cracks or large gaps where children threw rocks*. The reader can easily picture children throwing rocks to destroy the windows of this old, deserted house. The writer of Text Two also uses other details that fit very well with the horror or ghost genre that this kind of writing naturally belongs to, including the names *Reston Mansion*, or *the medium size[d] village of Whipville*, with villagers who love to spread rumours about an old, spooky house.

- Text One has chosen some good **vocabulary**, that helps the reader picture or hear the place or object being described; the verbs *rustling* and *moaning* are just right to create a quiet but eerie sound at the beginning of the piece, and the verbs *crunched* and *squeaked*, again, are just right to create a small sudden sound that would make you jump and so add to the tense atmosphere of the piece. The writer of Text Two chooses words well too. But what the writer of Text Two does particularly well is to put words together to create rich descriptive pictures, which are precise and focused. *The previously polished brass knocker was now a worn down rusty metal block hanging off the door.* In that one sentence there are two adjectival phrases: *previously polished* and *worn down*, two adjectives: *brass* and *rusty* and an adverbial phrase: *hanging off the door.* The writer also uses words, like *forbade* and *exterior*, *neglect* and *property* that sound formal and may even sound a little old-fashioned, which adds to the serious atmosphere of the piece of writing.

Look now in more detail at sentence level features:
- Both writers can use **full stops** and **capital letters** accurately almost all the time. All full stops and capital letters must be accurate for a Level 6⁺.
- Text One uses a **single comma** to separate one clause from another: *My friends go to 'the barn' every week, but Im disallowed* and also uses **commas in a pair**, to separate a phrase in the middle of a sentence: *The ashes were still there, an inch thick on the floor, but were very compressed.* This confidence at using commas is one of the features that make this piece a Level 5. The writer of Text One does make the occasional mistake; note the missing apostrophe from *I'm*. Text Two is also confident at using commas, singularly *Once the family fled, the dust began to settle* and in pairs *Now, with all the elegant vases and figurines, the warmth and homeliness of the mansion has been overcome by the cold and neglect.* The writer is also particularly good at using commas towards the beginning of a sentence after an opening word or phrase: *Inside, the once grand staircase ... In the kitchen, the radio ...* Being able to write with commas confidently and in a variety of ways is important to move toward writing at Level 6⁺.

● Text One and Text Two both use some **co-ordinate clauses**, starting with *and* or *but*. *It had boarded up windows <u>and</u> the floorboards squeaked* (Text One) and *the bed is neatly made <u>and</u> the hair brush on the table still holds the hairs . . .* (Text Two). The writer of Text One is beginning to use **subordinating connectives** to introduce **subordinate clauses**: *The sticks . . . crunch on the ground <u>when</u> you walk*. But the writer of Text One seems most confident using **co-ordinators** like *and* or *but*. The writer of Text Two uses a wider range of **subordinators**, such as *where, which, because* or *however*. For example: *The tiny bed, where the parents sang lullabies to the baby . . .* or, *The mirror is intact however the wardrobe has become damp from the weather*. The word *however*, which should have a comma before it, enables the writer to create a detailed picture of the wardrobe and its mirror.

● The writer of Text One **varies sentence length** effectively, another reason why the writing is given a Level 5. The writer uses a short sentence like *No-one ever went there* to make the reader stop and think about why that might be before describing the house. The use of plenty of co-ordinate clauses also ensures that there are lots of longer sentences to create a quiet, calm, if spooky atmosphere, where very little is happening. This is just right for a description of a house where there is nothing happening because it is so isolated! The writer of Text Two does not use very short sentences at all, but you could argue that the continuous use of longer sentences very forcefully builds up the sense of a still, lifeless place, where nothing has happened for years and years.

● There is much more variety of **sentence structure** in Text Two than in Text One. The writer of Text One relies on co-ordinating clauses a lot of the time, while the writer of Text Two is more adventurous in the sentence structures used. Notice how the writer starts this sentence with a subordinate clause: *Because of the viney weeds,* *the terracotta path could barely be visible.* This is effective because it makes us want to find out what *the viney weeds* have done to this house.

- This writer is also confident using the **passive voice** for effect: *a pile of newspapers can barely be recognised ...* (the active would be *you can hardly recognise a pile of newspapers*) or *the bed is neatly made ...* (the active would be *somebody had neatly made the bed*). This is effective because it throws the emphasis onto the main object in the sentence, the newspapers or the bed, by moving them to the beginning of the sentence. It also removes any mention of a person doing anything which also adds to the sense of an empty house where nobody has been, or done anything in it, for years.

- The writer of Text Two is very good at varying the beginnings of sentences with **adverbials** like *Inside, Upstairs, Now, In the kitchen.* In this sentence, *This was the maid's headquarters, now it is the headquarters of emptiness,* notice the repetition of the word *headquarters* to link the previous life of the house to its present state.

- Both writers use **paragraphs** effectively when changing topic. For example, the writer of Text One starts a new paragraph when changing from a description of the house to an explanation of the rumours told about it. The writer of Text Two uses each paragraph effectively to move to a different part of the house. Paragraph two starts with *The exterior*, paragraph three with *Inside*, and paragraph four with *The nursery upstairs*. It makes it very easy for the reader to follow the writer on the tour of the house that he or she gives us.

In conclusion, both writers are mainly accurate and are beginning to be quite skilled in their choices of description, vocabulary, and in the way they vary their sentence structure. However, the writer of Text Two deserves a Level 7, because of the way **description** is used to give a focused and precise picture, because of the number of **adjectives** and **adjectival** and **adverbial phrases** used, and because of the fluent use of a variety of **complex sentences**, including a wide range of **connectives** and confident use of the **passive voice** for effect.

Make a checklist

After you have discussed in detail the differences between these two texts, work with a partner to make a 'Level 6[+] Checklist'. What things do you need to remember when you are trying to raise your writing from Level 5 to Level 6[+]? Make a list covering whole-text features and sentence features.

Note that your checklist will be a general one, giving an overall idea of what you need to aim at for Level 6[+]. In the units that follow, you will:

- look in detail at a range of writing types
- think about the features of each type of writing
- check your own writing against the features that you need to use
- track your improvements in the course of the unit.

Bear in mind that the examples which you have seen so far were written under test conditions. While you, too, will have to write under test conditions, most of your work at Key Stage 3 will be drafted. You can therefore develop ideas in detail, and work on getting punctuation correct. Aim, too, to regularly review and edit your writing, consciously focusing on trying to apply some of the techniques that you learn about. For example, most students who are aiming for Level 6[+] need to be imaginative and confident in the way they vary sentence structure and use vocabulary to add to the impact of their writing. This book does not deal with spelling, but you must take care to check your spelling. This will help you to achieve a sound Level 6[+] in your writing.

Above all, keep checking. Each unit which follows will help you make a checklist of the writing features covered. If you have a checklist in your mind of the features that you should be including, you will be in control of what you are doing. And if you are in control, you will succeed. We wish you success with this process.

Unit One

Writing to imagine, explore, entertain

In this unit, you will:

- **think about what is special about writing to imagine, explore, entertain**

- **review your own writing, to see what needs to be done to make it a sound Level 6^{+}**

- **look at how professional authors write stories to imagine, explore, entertain**

- **draft your own writing in this form.**

Main National Framework Objectives Covered: 7Wd14, 7Sn1, 7Sn2, 7Wr5, 8Wd11, 8Sn2, 8Wr6, 9Wd7, 9Sn1, 9Sn2, 9Wr5

Writing to imagine, explore, entertain – what is it?

This kind of writing describes an experience, an event, a person or a place. It might be about something that has actually happened, it might be based on fact, or it might be something fictional, created by the writer. Writing to imagine, explore and entertain makes the reader imagine something, picture something, or feel something. If the writing describes an exciting event, it should make the reader imagine that they are there. If the writing describes a person, it should make the reader feel that they can see that person, and know what they are like.

● The writer should help the reader **imagine** what someone else's experience is like, or what a place is like. Evocative descriptions and effective use of imagery will help the reader to visualise a person, situation or setting.

● The writer should help the reader **explore** the thoughts and feelings of the characters in the writing. This can be conveyed through using an appropriate narrative style, to suit the writer's purpose. It can also be conveyed through dialogue; through the characters' responses to what happens to them; through the way in which the author describes the characters and their thoughts and feelings; and through the imagery associated with the characters.

● The reader should feel **entertained** and gripped by the writing, wanting to find out what happens to the people they are reading about. We should respond to the characters, and be able to to relate to some or dislike some. We should feel satisfied that the writing is credible or believable, and that we have experienced a range of emotions through our reading that we may not necessarily have experienced ourselves.

Here are some examples of writing to imagine, explore and entertain:

narratives   diaries

peoms

descriptions of places
or characters

play scripts

autobiographies

biography

letters to friends

newspaper reports

travel writing

jokes

 Can you think of any other kinds of writing that are meant to imagine, explore and entertain?

What makes a good piece of writing to imagine, explore, entertain?

So how can you be successful as a writer, in helping your reader to picture what you describe, or in grabbing and holding their attention?

Here are some of the **features** of writing to imagine, explore and entertain.

In groups, put the following features in rank order. Which are the most important features in making a piece of writing successful? Why is each important? How will it help the reader?

- a good opening
- engaging narrative style
- use of a range of narrative devices
- experimenting with multiple narratives
- shifts in timescale
- interesting and plausible characters
- being able to draw inferences from characters' actions and responses
- being able to empathise with the characters
- detailed descriptions
- morals or lessons about life
- effective and precise vocabulary
- imagery that creates vivid pictures in the reader's mind
- lots of action
- dialogue that helps us understand characters
- dialogue that is succinct and relevant
- suspense
- effective closure
- variety in the sentence structure and length
- accurate spelling, punctuation and paragraphing.

Compare your list with the lists made by other people. Do other groups agree with your rank order? Why? Work with your teacher to make a whole-class rank order, with reasons, of the features that a successful piece of writing to imagine, explore and entertain should have. Write your final list, with the reasons, into your notebook.

How can you improve your own writing?

Collect two or three pieces of your own writing to imagine, explore and entertain. Talk to your partner. How many of the features do you use already? What features do you need to improve?

On this and the following pages, there are grids that show in detail the things you need to do for a sound Level 6⁺. There are a lot of things to think about, but don't worry. A lot of them you will already be doing well. Some, though, you will need to improve. The grids will help you think about which areas you need to improve. If you are not sure about a feature, your teacher will be able to explain. You could also wait to see how the feature is used later in the unit.

Copy the grids into your notebook. (It may also be possible for your teacher to photocopy them.) For each feature, put a tick in the box which applies to you. When you have finished, you will be able to see what aspects of your work you need to focus on in the rest of this unit. You will then be able to track your targets and improvements as you write.

FEATURES OF WRITING	I can do this sometimes	I can usually do this	I need to improve this
I engage my reader's interest with an effective opening that raises questions.			
I give the reader clues about complications that could be developed later.			
I use a range of narrative styles and perspectives (third-person omniscient narrator or first-person interior monologue).			
I organise my work effectively, with interesting openings, good links between ideas and effective closure/endings.			
I explore relationships between characters and my characters are credible.			
I use dialogue, which is correctly punctuated, to give clues about characters.			
I experiment with imagery to convey character and setting.			

FEATURES OF WRITING	I can do this sometimes	I can usually do this	I need to improve this
I sequence my ideas into paragraphs (using time/topic/talk and narrative viewpoint to structure my writing).			
I develop my ideas, using adverbials and expanded noun phrases to add detail.			
I use repetition to emphasise key ideas or themes.			
I use the passive to create an impersonal style or to add emphasis.			
I vary my sentence structure, using simple, compound and complex sentences.			
I vary the position of subordinate clauses in my sentences.			
I vary my sentence length to create particular effects.			
I use unconventional sentence structures where appropriate.			
I use a range of punctuation correctly (including commas, semi-colons and colons) and vary my punctuation.			
I punctuate subordinate clauses within sentences correctly.			
I use the correct verb form and tense throughout my writing, changing tense for specific reasons.			
I employ a range of stylistic devices (including patterning, contrasts, tense changes).			
I use language precisely to create particular effects and shades of meaning.			
I choose my vocabulary carefully and use abstract nouns, non-finite verbs, adverbs and adjectives for effect.			

FEATURES OF WRITING	I can do this sometimes	I can usually do this	I need to improve this
I craft my writing and edit it carefully, taking my reader into consideration.			
I re-read my work, and revise style, structure and accuracy carefully.			
I spell most words accurately, including more complex words.			
I keep lists of words I misspell and learn how to spell these correctly, applying spelling patterns where possible.			
I edit my work carefully, to check the spellings I am unsure about.			

Now identify statements you wish to target in order to reach a Level 6+ in your writing. Write these into your writing journal. Review your progress regularly as you work through the unit.

How do they do it?

Two different openings of stories

As discussed in the earlier two books in this series, the opening of any writing is important: the writer needs to involve the reader, set the scene, and make the reader interested enough to continue reading. The reader needs to imagine the situation, start to explore some of the feelings of the characters, and be entertained by the text.

We are going to examine two different openings to novels, with different examples of narrative style. This is to explore a range of features that contribute towards a successful introduction to a story. It is also to allow you to make choices about which style you want to use for particular purposes.

Coram Boy by Jamila Gavin

In her introduction to her book, Jamila Gavin explains that it was based on fact: the plight of orphan children in the eighteenth century. According to local belief at that time, the 'Coram man' collected abandoned children, supposedly to take them into care. However, this was not true. The man either sold the children into slavery or left them to die. Eventually, in 1741, Captain Thomas Coram opened a hospital to care for children. The *Coram Boy* is the story of a child who was lucky: he was rescued, unlike many others at the time.

In this novel, Jamila Gavin writes as an omniscient narrator (an all-seeing narrator), using a third-person narrative style. Thus, the author is not directly involved in the story, but is describing what happens from an outside perspective.

'Oi! Meshak! Wake up, you lazy dolt!' The sound of the rough voice set the dogs barking. 'Can't you see one of the panniers is slipping on that mule there! Not that one, you nincompoop,' as the boy leapt guiltily from the wagon and darted in an agitated way among the overloaded animals, 'that one – there – fifth one back! Yes. Fool of a boy. Why was I so cursed with a son like you? I don't have to have eyes in the back of my head to know that one of the mules had his load slipping. What goes on inside that addled brain of yours?'

The author involves the reader in the text immediately and engages our interest by using a range of strategies:

● The **dialogue** used indicates the character of the speaker. Note the way in which he calls his son: *Oi!* This rough address to his son, and the insults he uses: *lazy dolt, nincompoop, fool of a boy, addled brain*, all reveal what sort of person he is. What do these insults show the reader about the speaker's personality and his attitude to his son? Although we've heard his voice, we haven't yet been introduced to him: he's Otis, the main villain in the story.

● Note the interesting variety of **punctuation** used by the author:
  ■ There are lots of **exclamation marks** and several **rhetorical questions** (questions

which are not answered). Why have these been used? What is their effect?

■ Look again at the sentence which has **dashes** in it. Say this sentence out loud. What is the effect of the dashes?

● The dialogue also includes some examples of **unconventional sentence structure**: *Yes. Fool of a boy.* These are unusual because they are incomplete sentences. What has been left out? What is the effect of this?

● The author's **vocabulary choice** is effective: Meshak *leapt guiltily* and *darted in an agitated way.* What do the verbs, *leapt* and *darted*, imply about Meshak's character and his attitude towards Otis? Notice, too, the adverb, *guiltily,* and the adjective, *agitated*, both of which also reveal the effect Otis has on Meshak. It is far more effective for readers to infer aspects of someone's character from the author's description of them and their responses, than to have their character described in an obvious way for readers.

Reader response

How do you respond to the two characters presented in this opening paragraph? With whom do you sympathise? What questions about the characters, their background, or their motives, have been raised for you? How do you think the author wanted you to feel about the characters? Find a quotation to support how you feel about each of the two characters. If your interest has been engaged and issues have been raised, then this is an effective opening paragraph.

It's your turn

You are now going to write your own opening to a story which engages the reader and introduces them to two of your main characters through dialogue. Think about two people who have different characters. What are they like? What are they doing? What is their relationship? How do they feel about each other? What are they saying to each other? Who is the dominant character? How does he or she speak? How does the other character respond? Try to visualise the situation and feel the atmosphere between the two people.

Think about your vocabulary carefully. Your selection of what to describe, and what to include in the dialogue, will determine how much you need to tell your readers and how much your readers will be able to work out for themselves. Remember, it is better to imply character through actions, thoughts, body language and responses, that to tell the readers everything about your characters directly.

You will use a third-person narrative style (as though you are watching the scene, but not directly involved in it). You also need to focus on using dialogue, as Jamila Gavin did, to reveal character and their attitudes.

Now write your opening passage.

Editing your work

Work with a response partner, to check the following aspects of your work:

- Does your dialogue reveal **aspects of character**? Have you a balance between aspects of character that have been explicitly described, and aspects that your reader needs to infer from your descriptions? Does your partner respond to your characters in the way you had hoped?
- Have you **punctuated your dialogue** accurately?
- Have you used a **range of punctuation**?
- Have you included some **unconventional sentence structures**? What is the effect of these?
- Have you focused on the quality and precision of your **vocabulary choices**?

After the First Death by Robert Cormier

A bus full of young children is hijacked one morning and the hijackers demand that unless their ultimatums are met, the children will be killed. This novel has a very different narrative style to the previous one. It has shifting viewpoints, as well as a dual narrative (two parallel stories). The story of the hijack is recounted by a third-person narrator, and the story of Ben, the general's son, is written in interior monologue or a stream of consciousness style. The story opens with the voice of Ben.

I keep thinking that I have a tunnel in my chest. The path the bullet took, burrowing through the flesh and sinew and whatever muscle the bullet encountered (I am not the macho muscled type, not at five eleven and one hundred eighteen pounds). Anyway, the bullet went through my chest and out again. The wound has healed and there is no pain. The two ends of the tunnel are closed although there's a puckering of the skin at both ends of the tunnel. And a faint redness. The puckering has a distinct design, like the old vaccination scar on my father's arm. Years from now, the wound will probably hurt the way my father's old wounds hurt him, the wounds he received in those World War Two battles. My mother always jokes about the wounds: oh, not the wounds themselves but the fact that he professes to forecast weather by the phantom pains and throbbings in his arms and legs.

Will my wound ache like his when I am his age?

And will I be able to tell when the rain will fall by the pain whistling through the tunnel in my chest?

Your first responses

Work with a partner to identify ways in which this first-person interior monologue is **different in style** to the previous extract from *Coram Boy*. What features do you notice that are particular to this extract? To get you started, look at features such as pronouns, the content of the passage, and the use of dialogue and thoughts. List the features of this extract. How do you feel when you read this account? In what ways is this response different to how you felt when you read the previous extract? How does the content differ from the previous opening passage? Think about the match between the content of the passages, and the style of each. What do you notice?

How the author does it

Because we read Ben's thoughts directly, we feel closer to him: it's as though we are actually hearing his thoughts or reading his diary. We are less conscious of the author 'crafting' the passage and feel more directly involved with the character. There are various ways in which Cormier achieves this:

- He uses a **parenthetic aside** (the aside in brackets, like an added afterthought):
  (*I am not the macho muscled type, not at five eleven and one hundred eighteen pounds*).
  What is the effect of this technique? What extra details do you learn about Ben and how he feels about himself? Using either brackets or a pair of commas as parenthesis is a very useful way of addressing the reader directly.

- The extract has a **conversational style**, indicated by the use of the adverb *anyway* and the interjection *oh*. This makes it feel as though Ben is talking to us directly. Try to identify a range of other words or phrases writers use to achieve the same effect.

- There is **unconventional sentence structure**: *And a faint redness*. What is missing from this sentence? What is the effect of the sentence?

- There is **repetition** of *wound*, both Ben's and his father's. Usually writers try to vary their vocabulary, but here Cormier has deliberately used the noun six times in three consecutive sentences. Why do you think he does this? What is the effect?

- The **figurative language** used by Ben to describe his wound helps us to visualise it. For example, look again at the **metaphor** of the tunnel: *And will I be able to tell when the rain will fall by the pain whistling through the tunnel in my chest?* What image comes to your mind when you read that sentence? Which words in particular help to create the image for you?

- The extract ends with two **rhetorical questions**. What is the effect of these?

- The passage is **personal** and **reflective**. It's as though Ben is sharing his views directly with the reader. Consequently, we are drawn into the account. We may also have several questions that we hope will be answered during the novel. Write two or three questions that you would like the text to answer.

It's your turn

You are now going to write your own opening to a story which engages the reader and introduces them to one of your main characters through an interior monologue or stream of consciousness style. Think about someone who is facing a difficult time, or someone who has an important decision to make. What has happened to him or her? How has your character responded to what has happened? Is he or she bitter, angry, accepting, dejected, frustrated, excited or optimistic? How else may the person be feeling? Is your character experiencing a range of emotions? Are some of these conflicting emotions? What options face this person? Try to visualise the situation and recreate the thoughts of your character. Remember to try to capture their thoughts as they are going through their head, so that your reader is able to share these, and gain an insight into what your character feels. (Alternatively, you could rewrite your first opening passage – from the work based on *Coram Boy* – as an interior monologue, from the point of view of one of the characters involved.)

Now write your opening passage.

Editing your work

Work with a response partner, to check the following aspects of your work:

- Does your writing convey the **situation** the person is experiencing accurately?
- Have you included **parenthesis**? Have you used a conversational style?
- Have you included some **unconventional sentence structures**? What is the effect of these?
- Is there **repetition** of a central concern or idea that is occupying your character's thoughts?
- Have you used **imagery** to help your reader to visualise what your character is feeling?
- Have you focused on the quality and precision of your **vocabulary choices**?
- Have you used a **range of punctuation**?
- Does your partner respond to your characters in the way you had hoped?
- Is your partner interested in reading further? Is he or she left with a range of questions that they hope will be answered in your story?

The more you are able to include features from the checklists provided in your work, the closer to Level 6+ your writing will be.

Now review what you have learnt in the opening section of this unit. When would you choose to use a third-person narrative style? And when would you choose to use an interior monologue or stream of consciousness style? List the main features of each.

How do they do it?

More about people and places

As in *After the First Death*, *Coram Boy* also has a dual narrative. This is when there are two parallel stories running throughout the novel; the reader only discovers the link between the two threads of the story towards the end.

You've already met Meshak in *Coram Boy*. The other son in the parallel thread of the story is Alexander. In the extract that follows, Thomas, who is to become Alexander's friend, is the new boy at school. Thomas is being bullied by the others:

It all changed suddenly. One night, Thomas was hanging by a rope, upside down from the beam, when he became aware of Alexander watching from a corner. He lounged against one of the wooden posts as if he were carved out of it, half in shadow, his face chiselled into a mask. Only his eyes glimmered darkly. He did nothing while two, three times, the boys twisted the rope then let it go, so that he spun fiercely like a top, helpless, dizzy, sick, while the boys laughed uproariously. Alexander's movement was unexpected. Even his torturers paused and turned. As if to show he was one of the lads, Alexander came forward. He grabbed Thomas's wrist and roughly tied one of the knots but, while doing so, he whispered in his ear, 'Make them laugh. If you can make them laugh, they'll never trouble you again.'

- Note the **variation in sentence length** throughout this paragraph. Count the long and short sentences, and note where they are placed in the paragraph. Now note what is happening in each of these sentences. This variation in sentence length is effective as it develops tension and sustains interest.
  - Consider the effect of the short opening sentence of the paragraph: *It all changed suddenly* and the fourth sentence of the extract: *Only his eyes glimmered darkly.* How do you feel when you read these sentences? What do you expect to happen?
  - Now compare this with the long sentence describing Thomas spinning: *He did nothing while two, three times, the boys twisted the rope then let it go, so that he spun fiercely like a top, helpless, dizzy, sick, while the boys laughed uproariously.* What is the effect of the longer sentence? What does the regular use of commas do to the pace of the sentence? How does this help us to understand what Thomas was experiencing?

- Notice the effective **vocabulary**. The **verbs** used to describe Alex's features are very precise: *his face chiselled into a mask* and *his eyes glimmered darkly.* What impression does each verb give you? Why do you feel this way? Think about the connotations (or associations) of each verb. Notice also, the **contrast** between the stony, chilled features of his face and his gleaming eyes. What feeling does that give you? Here, Jamila Gavin has effectively conveyed just how intensely Alexander feels through her descriptive detail.

We have considered how one author has developed aspects of character for the reader. Similar strategies are also used to describe places.

Later, Thomas goes home with Alexander for a visit. On the way to Alexander's house they encounter Meshak and Otis. Meshak becomes fascinated with the house and its occupants, and spends hours staring at it:

The moon was hugely bright, gibbous and almost menacing. Its reflection made the lake mercurial. Dark clouds flared across the sky like horses' tails and he saw how fierce the wind was by the way the trees swayed.

As he watched, a movement caught his eye. Someone stood on the lawn outside, staring at an upstairs window of the house; a raggle-taggle fellow. With the clouds trailing across the moon, Thomas kept losing him in the shadows, then there he was again; a youth, barely older than himself, he thought, standing stock-still, his legs apart, his arms slightly akimbo, like some half-formed statue. Thomas felt he had seen him before but had barely time to register the figure as the moon disappeared completely and darkness swallowed him up. When the clouds parted again, the fellow had gone.

Thomas shuddered. Filled with unease, he closed the shutters.

Consider the following aspects of the way in which the author has crafted the passage:

- Notice how atmosphere is created through the author's use of **personification**. For example, the author describes the moon as *almost menacing* and the darkness is described as swallowing the figure on the lawn. How do these examples of personification make you feel? Why?

- **Sentence structure**, **punctuation** and **variation in sentence length** are all used to good effect.
  - Note the length of the third sentence of the second paragraph of the extract: *With the clouds trailing across the moon, Thomas kept losing him in the shadows, then there he was again; a youth, barely older than himself, he thought, standing stock-still, his legs apart, his arms slightly akimbo, like some half-formed statue.* Why do you think the author included this long sentence at this point? What is happening in the passage that the lengthy sentence echoes or reflects?
  - Notice, too, the use of the **semi-colon** in the above sentence. This form of punctuation serves to join the two linked ideas. It is stronger than a comma, yet not as strong as a full stop, thus indicating the close relationship and equal balance between the two parts of the sentence. Can you identify another place in the paragraph just quoted where a semi-colon could have been used instead of a comma or full stop? Why did the author choose her original form of punctuation at this point? Can you think of a rule to help you to choose when to use a semi-colon in your writing?

● Placement of **non-finite clauses**. Notice how at the end of the extract the clause *filled with unease* comes before the subject and main clause of the sentence. What is the effect of this? This is a useful technique whenever you wish to emphasise the atmosphere that has been created.

● **Expansion of noun phrases**. Look again at that lengthy sentence in the second paragraph: *a youth, <u>barely older than himself</u>, he thought, <u>standing stock-still, his legs apart, his arms slightly akimbo, like some half-formed statue</u>.* The underlined sections are all examples of expanded noun phrases to describe the youth. What is the effect of this cumulative description? What does it add to the passage?

the clouds . . . flared across the sky like horses' tails

● **Contrasts** are also used to excellent effect. Note the contrast between the **movement** of the natural elements: the changeable lake, the clouds, which *flared across the sky like horses' tails*, and the fierce wind; and the **stillness** of the figure on the lawn: *standing stock-still . . . like some half-formed statue*. Why has the author included these contrasts? What do they serve to emphasise?

the moon was hugely bright, gibbous and almost menacing

Explanations about sentence structures to help you

The **variety of sentence structures** used reveal the author's ability to craft language effectively. Writers use a variety of simple sentences, compound sentences and complex sentences.

- **Simple** sentences are sentences with only one clause: *Make them laugh.*

- **Compound** sentences are sentences made up of simple sentences joined by co-ordinating conjunctions, such as *and, but, or.* Compound sentences are useful. They allow us to make simple links between ideas and they give equal value to the different clauses in the sentence: *He grabbed Thomas's hand and roughly tied one of the knots* . . . Both actions are important. The *and* tells us that one followed quickly after the other.

- **Complex** sentences give additional information; they also indicate the relationship between ideas. Each one has a main clause and at least one subordinate clause. Look at the following examples, and explain how you can tell the difference between a main clause and a subordinate (or dependent) clause.

Examples of complex sentences:

As if to show he was one of the lads, <u>Alexander came forward</u>.
    (*subordinate clause*)   (main clause)

If you can make them laugh, <u>they'll never trouble you again</u>.
    (*subordinate clause*)   (main clause)

<u>Thomas was hanging by a rope</u> *when he became aware of Alexander watching.*
    (main clause)   (*subordinate clause*)

<u>He did nothing</u> *while two, three times, the boys twisted the rope then let it go.*
  (main clause)   (*subordinate clause*)

Note the clauses in these examples: the main clause can always stand alone; it makes sense on its own, whereas the subordinate clause is dependent on the main clause for meaning. In these examples, the subordinate clause has been placed before or after the main clause. An alternative is to embed the subordinate clause in the main clause (to insert it into the main clause), as in the examples below:

Alexander, *as if to show he was one of the lads,* came forward.
        (*subordinate clause*)

<u>Thomas,</u> *when he became aware of Alexander watching,* <u>was hanging by a rope.</u>
        (*subordinate clause*)

Subordinators

To form a subordinate clause, you need to use a subordinator. Some of the most frequent subordinators are:

- **subordinating conjunctions:**
  because, if, although, unless, while, since, as, whenever, whereas, though, after, before, once, until, than, that, in case.

- **relative pronouns:**
  which, that, whose.

Time to practise

Write two sentences (or clauses) and combine them to form a complex sentence. Vary the position of the subordinate clause. Remember to try to place your subordinate clause at the start of the sentence, embedded within the main clause, and at the end of the sentence. Once you have written your sentences, consider the effect of the placement of the subordinate clause. Are there any rules you are able to identify? You may use your own sentences or you may combine the sentences which follow, to start you off:

The teacher gave us lots of homework. The class was disgruntled and reacted noisily.

The weather was gloomy, with fog, wind and rain. My family went on holiday to the coast.

Success is desirable. Success comes to those who work hard and focus on their goals.

It's your turn

You are now going to write again, concentrating on exploring people or a place in more detail. As before, use the extracts you have read and discussed (both now and earlier in the unit) as models for your own writing. The writing does not have to be lengthy; aim to write between one and three paragraphs.

Reflect

Before you start, remind yourself of your targets for this unit of work. Review your opening passages you wrote, as well as the evaluation from your work with your response partner. Aim to make this short piece of writing better than your earlier one, particularly in terms of vocabulary, punctuation, imagery, sentence construction and sentence length.

Write your extract, ensuring that you include at least one example of each of the three sentence structures described: simple, compound and complex. If you have more than one complex sentence, try to vary where you place your subordinate clause: aim to start with the subordinate clause, embed it within the main clause, or add it after the main clause.

Check the following:

- Have you varied your sentence length? Where the sentence length has changed, what is the reason for this?
- Have you varied the structure of your sentences, including using complex sentences and changing the position of the subordinate clause? Have you started a sentence with a non-finite clause? Can you explain the effect of the sentence choices you have made?
- Is your vocabulary precise, rich and interesting?
- Have you used figurative language or symbolism? How does this add to the atmosphere you wish to create?
- Is there an opportunity to include a contrast, to add emphasis?
- Have you included a range of punctuation (commas, semi-colons, colons, dashes, exclamation marks, questions marks) to help your reader make sense of your meaning?
- Have you addressed your targets for this piece of writing?

Ask a response partner to read your work and comment on the above aspects. Is there anything else they value in your writing? Is there anything they recommend you change?

Redraft any sections of your work that still need further improvement.

Reflect again

What progress have you made towards reaching your targets? What progress have you made since starting this unit of work? How clear, precise, varied and rich is your writing? Write a self-evaluative comment in your notebook, recording the progress towards reaching your targets that you have made. Include aspects that you still wish to target further.

The middle of your story: the development or complication

This next extract is again taken from *Coram Boy*, by Jamila Gavin. Alexander has been evicted from his father's house because of their conflict over Alexander's chosen career:

Everyone was affected by the gloom that hung over the house; it billowed around like a great fog, in which people and objects lost their identity and become just disembodied shapes. Tension and suppressed anger were as palpable as a storm brewing in the hills, when sheep huddle together and cattle make for the shelter of the trees, when dogs bark meaninglessly and flocks of birds fly in confused circles in the sky.

- **Figurative language** or **imagery** (in the form of **similes**) creates vivid pictures in the reader's mind. What is the gloom compared with? How is this image developed in the second sentence, with the analogy of the storm brewing? What is the effect on the reader?

- **Use of senses**: the author develops the atmosphere through using a combination of senses, and relying on more than sense to help the reader to visualise the scene.
  - Sight becomes blurred in the fog/gloom – people and objects become *disembodied shapes*.
  - Touch is implied. It's as though the tension can be felt in the way the atmosphere is compared to a brewing storm, particularly with the word *palpable* (which means able to be touched, felt, or perceived).
  - Noise is suggested with the description *when dogs bark meaninglessly*.
  What is the effect of using a range of senses?

- **Use of passive**: the author emphasises the effect of the atmosphere on everyone in the house by using the passive form, which places the object of the sentence at the start of the sentence: *Everyone was affected by the gloom that hung over the house ...* Using the active form here would have emphasised the atmosphere instead. For example: *The gloom that hung over the house affected everyone.*

- **Expansion of noun phrases**: This is another characteristic of an able writer. Look at the following example: *the gloom <u>that hung over the house</u>*. Can you work out an explanation of what an expanded noun phrase is? How is this more effective than using a noun on its own, or a noun preceded by adjectives? Adjectives are usually placed before the noun they describe. You may come up with several reasons for using a noun phrase like this. For example, using the noun phrase after the noun adds variety to sentences; it emphasises the noun (*gloom*); and gives additional detail to give the reader a fuller picture.

Similarly, in *After the First Death* the environment reflects the atmosphere and feelings of the characters. In this extract, Kate, the young girl who is driving the bus at the time of the kidnapping incident, is feeling suffocated inside the hot, stuffy bus:

The long afternoon burned on, the heat increasing, pounding at the taped windows, pressing on the roof of the bus like a giant's hot hand. The helicopters came and went, roaring and throbbing and fluttering and then receding, fading away; and after a while, Kate discerned a pattern in their arrivals and departures. Every fifteen minutes. Occasionally, a siren howled, piercing the air with its sound of emergency: something gone wrong, something gone askew. Distant shouts sometimes reached them, and Kate would press eager eyes to the window slits but would see no movement out there, no activity, the woods shrouded and still. Yet, the helicopters and sirens were reminders that someone was out there, someone was watching. But what could they do as long as the hijackers held the children?

- **Figurative language** is used to excellent effect in this extract. The afternoon heat has been **personified**. What does the author, Cormier, compare the heat to? What feeling does this give you? Describing the noise of the siren as a *howl* is also powerful. What image does this evoke? What feelings are aroused in the reader?

- **Repetition** of central ideas helps to reinforce the effect of this being an overwhelming, relentless experience. What sense, or feeling, is created by the repetition of the nouns *something* and *someone*?

- **A build-up or accumulation of adjectives** (*roaring, throbbing, fluttering, receding, fading*), again suggests the continual nature of the noises surrounding Kate. The rhythm and volume of the sentence, created by the different strengths of the adjectives, connotes (suggests) the varying tones of the helicopters, depending on how close to the bus they were.

- **Unconventional sentence structure** is used for emphasis or impact. Can you find a sentence that is unconventional or incomplete? What is missing? What is the effect of this?

- **Noun phrases**: What is the difference between placing the description of the noun before the noun, for example: *the shrouded and still woods,* and placing it after the noun, as Robert Cormier has done: *the woods shrouded and still?*

- This **third-person narrative style** is very different from the opening paragraph quoted from the same novel (Ben's interior monologue) on page 10. Cormier adopts a different narrative technique for different sections of the text, allowing the two narrative threads of the novel to each have their own distinct 'voice' and style. This is a useful technique to adopt if you wish to have two parallel threads to your story. There are similarities with the internal monologue, though. For example, the **rhetorical question** at the end of the paragraph draws the reader in to share Kate's concerns.

An explanation of adverbials to help you

Adverbials can describe the time, place or manner of an event. Like subordinate clauses, their position within a sentence can vary, depending on the effect you wish to create. For example, placing an adverbial at the start of a sentence brings it to the foreground of the reader's imagination and therefore adds emphasis to that part of the sentence. When you write, practise placing adverbials in different parts of your sentences and reflect on the effect this creates.

Examples of adverbials:

Spot the patterns in these examples of adverbials.

- to tell us more about **when**/the **time** something happened:
  Tension and suppressed anger were as palpable as a storm brewing in the hills, <u>when sheep huddle together and cattle make for the shelter of the trees</u> ...

- to tell us more about **where**/the **place** something happened:
  The long afternoon burned on, the heat increasing, pounding <u>at the taped windows</u>, pressing <u>on the roof of the bus</u> ...

- to tell us more about **how**/the **manner** in which something happened:
  The long afternoon burned on, the heat increasing, pounding at the taped windows, pressing on the roof of the bus <u>like a giant's hot hand</u>.

Note that the adverbials each start with an adverb or a preposition, placed before the noun phrase.

Now think of your own examples, following the pattern given:

Main clause (subject + verb)	Adverbial
The heat increased, pounding	(time) in time with the throb of the helicopter blades
The heat increased, pounding	(place) against my bruised and weary head
The heat increased, pounding	(manner) like an angry god, woken from his sleep

It's your turn

In pairs or small groups, **discuss** the two extracts. Focus on:

- the ways in which the authors have used the atmosphere to reflect the conflict experienced by the characters
- the ways in which the authors have extended their ideas (for example, through using adverbials or expanded noun phrases)
- the similarities and differences between the extracts.

Reflect

Think about your original targets for this unit, plus targets that arose from your last piece of writing. Consider the ways in which you could meet these targets in your next piece of writing. Consider, too, how using figurative language can help you to create vivid, rich images for your reader. Think about ways in which the authors have added detail and interest to their descriptions; are there models you could adapt for your own writing?

Write your own account of a complication in a situation – one in which conflict between characters escalates and is reflected in the atmosphere created. If you wish, you could continue the story given in one of the extracts. Think carefully about the imagery you are going to use, your vocabulary, and the ways in which you are going to develop your descriptions. How will you draw the reader into the experience you are describing?

Ask a response partner to read over your work for you, while you read theirs. Which parts are particularly good? Which parts are less effective? Use the checklists given earlier, as well as the ideas you have generated from your discussion, to suggest ways in which you think you could each improve your work.

Redraft the parts of your writing which you or your partner highlighted as needing additional work. Is there anything else you need to revise in order to meet your targets for this piece of writing?

Aspects to target further? Successes? Targets?

Reflect again

By now you should have had the opportunity to practise writing in ways that will help you to meet several of your targets for improving your writing. How much progress have you made? How close are you to that next target level? What aspects of your work are you most proud of? What areas do you still need to address in more detail?

Write a self-evaluative comment, reflecting on your progress so far.

How to end a story

Coram Boy

Today, he carried on quickly as if to escape from the crying voices mingling with the piercing trill of the skylark; past the cottage until the woods gave way to pastures. He leant on the stile and looked across to the Ashbrook orphanage. His eyes followed the fields hazy with barley; across the meadow where slender horses cast long-legged shadows as they moved, sleek and slow, cropping at the sweet grass. He gazed tenderly on his mother, Lady Ashbrook, shepherding her orphans who clustered around her, clutching her skirts as if she were their own mother. Thank God for her, thank God for Captain Coram, who had saved so many little children. Yet just to see them brought a shudder too, for the shadow of Otis Gardiner still lingered and encircled the world like a menacing whirlwind, whose terror had never been harnessed, and who had never been caught to face justice.

- The **repetition** of *Thank God* in Alexander's thoughts suggests how fervently (strongly) he feels about the plight of the children. The caring attitude shown by both Alexander and his mother **contrast** with the uncaring attitude displayed by Otis in the opening passage of the novel.

- The **expanded noun phrase**: *Captain Coram, <u>who had saved so many little children,</u>* refers back to the title of the book, and reminds us of how many children also weren't saved. Thus, there is a satisfying sense of progress having been made.

- Look particularly at the concluding sentence of the paragraph.
  - The **connective** *yet* indicates a contrasting idea: although appreciative and positive in the preceding sentence, Alexander is also still unhappy. Why is this?
  - The **simile** *the shadow of Otis Gardiner still lingered and encircled the world like a menacing whirlwind . . .* is particularly effective. What does it suggest about Otis? The use of a shadow is symbolic, too. What are the connotations, or associations, of a shadow?
  - The **verbs**, *lingered* and *encircled*, have been chosen specifically. What do they convey?

- **Realism**: Do you remember the opening paragraph of the novel, where we were introduced to the villain, Otis, through his dialogue (see page 7)? In this resolution of the novel (the conclusion) we learn that the power of Otis over others has been diminished, and yet there is a recognition that it has not ended completely – just as evil is still a presence in our society. This is a realistic, or plausible ending because, although the situation has been resolved positively, it is not a 'happy ever after' situation; the reader is reminded of the potential for evil in mankind, as represented by Otis. One of the characteristics that makes this an effective part of the ending is the link with the opening, through the echoing of character.

It's your turn

Your task now is to write a realistic ending to the conflict situation you described earlier, resolving the crisis in the form of a satisfying closure. Try to visualise the complication you were asked to write earlier in the unit. How could this be resolved in a satisfying, yet realistic way? How are the characters feeling? What has happened since you last wrote to have caused them to feel this way? Is there some imagery which reflects their feelings? Think carefully about the precision of your vocabulary choices.

Follow the same procedure as before: reflect – write – check/review with a response partner – redraft – reflect again. When you write this time, try to incorporate as many of the ideas you've learnt during the course of working through this unit as possible.

When planning the **content** of your ending, or closure, aim to include several of the following features:

- echoes of character and character development
- echoes of themes
- contrasts with the opening
- symbolism or imagery
- an element of realism.

When you focus on the **style** of your writing, remember to include aspects targeted during this unit. Remember to:

- use expanded noun phrases and adverbials, to develop your descriptions
- use precise vocabulary choices, focusing on the connotations or associations of the words you select
- use a variety of sentence structures, and experiment with the placement of parts of sentences
- vary your sentence length for particular effects
- focus on using a range of punctuation, to support your reader, and complement meaning
- if appropriate, include carefully selected and correctly punctuated dialogue
- think carefully about the narrative style you select, and the reasons for this.

Don't forget to use a response partner to help with the editing of your work. Try, though, to work through your own editing process first, to give your partner your best version of your ending to read. The more of these aspects of writing you manage to include, the closer you will be to writing at a secure Level 6[+]! Remember, that the writing process is a conscious crafting and redrafting, and that writers – even professional ones – constantly look for ways in which to improve their work.

And you could try . . .

- Experiment with a range of different narrative techniques, such as withholding information, using time-shifts, writing a dual narrative.

- Write in a particular genre, and either exploit or parody the conventions of that genre. For example, you could write a twenty-first century version of a fairy-tale.

- Write the same story in a range of different genres and narrative styles. This is particularly useful for focusing on the impact of narrative choices made.

- Take a story you enjoyed writing earlier in the year, and rewrite it, applying several of the strategies you have learnt during the course of this unit.

- Write with attitude, from an unusual perspective. For example, you could be a cooker, writing about your view of the family with whom you live. You could explore your views of them, based on how they treat you and what you see happening in the kitchen. Or, you could be a motor vehicle, belonging to a particular member of the family.

- This unit has focused on fiction texts. There are also several examples of **non-fiction writing** which aim to imagine, explore and entertain. You could read some examples of journalistic writing or autobiographical writing, including travel writing, and then see how many of these techniques you have practised during the course of this unit apply to non-fiction writing too. Then, try to write your own article, autobiography or travelogue, which aims to imagine, explore and entertain.

- Alternatively, write a letter to a favourite niece or nephew, who is now five years old, for them to open when they turn sixteen. Your letter is going to try and provide some practical advice for them, but without sounding as though you are preaching to them. You will need to talk with wry humour about some of the life experiences you have had and hope that they will be able to apply lessons from your experiences.

Unit Two

Writing to inform, explain, describe

In this unit, you will:

- think about what is special about writing to inform, explain, describe

- review your own writing, to see what needs to be done to make it a sound Level 6$^+$

- look at how professional authors write natural history and autobiographical texts to inform, explain, describe

- draft your own writing in these forms.

Main National Framework Objectives Covered: 7Wd14, 7Wr14, 8Wd9, 8Wd11, 8Sn1, 8Sn2, 8Sn7, 8Wr11, 9Wd7, 9Sn2, 9Sn9, 9Wr9, 9Wr11

Writing to inform, explain, describe – what is it?

The majority of the writing you read in school (and out of school) is probably writing to **inform**, **explain** and **describe**. This writing covers a wide range of topics or subjects.

- Writing to **inform** gives you facts. It does not try to persuade you to follow one particular viewpoint or argument. For example, it may be writing you find in a Religious Studies textbook, such as *What is Buddhism?* You may find it on the Internet (e.g. when searching for information on *food suitable for hedgehogs*). You may also find it in a newspaper, for example, in an article entitled: *Ten outdoor activity summer holidays for teenagers*. It may be an advice leaflet from your doctor's surgery, about the signs and symptoms of meningitis. In each case the writer tells us information so we may find out new facts. This writing usually answers the questions: Who? What? Where? When?

- Writing to **explain** helps to make something plain or clear to the reader. For example, the writing may be explaining why soil erosion occurs, or what happens to the food we eat. The writer is usually explaining processes or difficult ideas. Often diagrams are used to support the explanation given in the body of the text. Explanations give us many facts. There may be more than one explanation or reason for an event, though, so writers then pick the most important information for the reader. For example, if we think about why soil erosion occurs we may come up with several reasons. These reasons will form part of the explanation. Writing to explain usually answers the questions why and how.

- Writing to **describe** often combines information and explanation. The writer describes what happened during a particular time or event. For example, they could write a description of life in India during the rainy season. They could also write a description of what happened during the World Cup, including what a particular football team felt about the event. This writing may answer a range of questions (including who, what, when, where, why, or how), depending on what the writer chooses to focus on. The writer selects what details to put into their description. Of the three forms of writing, descriptive writing is most likely to include adjectives, imagery and descriptive detail. You will also find lots of examples of descriptive writing in fiction texts that you read.

There are several overlaps between these forms of writing. A leaflet about a disease such as malaria, for example, may include information about symptoms. It may also explain what to do if you think you have the disease. It may also describe different types of malaria and where they are found. This kind of writing is rarely pure information, explanation or description. It is usually a mixture of text-types, with features of all three types of writing.

Discuss the following text-types. Which ones are meant to inform, explain and describe? Which ones have a combination of these types of writing? Discuss the list and see what you think.

a television programme about the possible effects of continued global warming

a newspaper article about how to help wild animals survive winter

a story about a refugee living in a refugee camp on the border of Afghanistan

an editorial about railway strikes

a letter from a soldier fighting in World War One

'the story of a chip: what happens once it's eaten'

a science fiction story

a private diary entry

a description of life in a Brazilian rain forest

an explanation of how hot-air balloons work

an encyclopaedia entry about walruses

an Internet site run by the 'Save the Dolphin' society

a leaflet entitled 'Drugs: their use and abuse'

an extract from a travel magazine about the Caribbean

a fantasy novel

an evaluation of your set design in Drama

a letter to the newspaper complaining about a new housing development

a leaflet from Greenpeace about why they are protesting against mining on the beaches

a journal entry entitled 'My trip to the North Pole – day 37'

an essay entitled 'The problems facing Zimbabwe'

an advertisement about a new shower gel

a letter about the new savings rates offered by a bank

a science experiment

your school report

What makes a good piece of writing to inform, explain, describe?

You now have an idea about the general features of writing to inform, explain and describe. You have also discussed some examples of these types of writing. For homework, collect as many different examples of these types of writing as you can. In this unit you will be focusing on natural history and autobiographical writing, so you should include those forms of writing in your sample. You will need to use a variety of sources to try and find as many different forms of this writing as possible. You could look in the following places:

- the Internet
- an encyclopaedia
- school textbooks (remember to look at writing in other subjects, not just English)
- non-fiction texts, such as autobiographies, travel writing, reportage, and subject-specific texts
- newspapers and magazines
- free information leaflets (available in supermarkets, Tourist Information Centres, DIY shops, pharmacies, doctors' surgeries, and so on)
- your own writing in a range of subjects.

 Working in groups, look at the examples you have collected. What **features** of writing to inform, explain and describe can you identify? Use your knowledge of non-fiction text-types to help you to identify key features at word, sentence and text level. Do you think that some of the group's examples are better than others? Can you explain why? Here are some ideas to help you to focus your discussion:

- Who is the **audience** for the writing? How do you know?
- How does the writer **catch our attention**?
- Is the writing clear, with effective use of **connectives** to link ideas? Collect examples of different ways in which the writers connect their ideas.
- Is the **vocabulary** varied and interesting? Has appropriate **subject-specific vocabulary** been used?
- Is the writing **well-structured** with varied sentence structures and sentence length?
- Is there appropriate use of **imagery**, to help you to visualise the situation?

How can you improve your own writing?

Collect two or three pieces of your own writing to inform, explain and describe. Remember to look at writing in other subjects as well as in English. Compare them with the two examples in the Students' Introduction. Talk to a partner about the things you do already. What things do you need to improve?

On this and the following pages, there are grids which show in detail the things you need to do to achieve a sound Level 6+. There are a lot of things to think about, but don't worry. A lot of them you will already be doing well. Some, though, you will need to improve. The grids will help you think about which areas you need to improve. If you are not sure about a feature, your teacher will be able to explain. You could also wait to see how the feature is used later in the unit.

Copy the grids into your notebook. (It may also be possible for your teacher to photocopy them.) For each feature, put a tick in the box which applies to you. When you have finished, you will be able to see what aspects of your work you need to focus on in the rest of this unit. You will then be able to track your targets and improvements as you write.

FEATURES OF WRITING	I can do this sometimes	I can usually do this	I need to improve this
I capture the reader's interest with an effective opening and engaging style.			
I write in a formal/impersonal or informal/personal style, as needed.			
I plan carefully and structure my writing so that the reader can make sense of my information, explanation or description.			
I use a range of paragraph structures, including one sentence paragraphs, if appropriate.			
I explain clearly and confidently so that the reader understands my explanation and my writing is credible.			
I combine information, explanation and description to give my reader a good understanding of my subject.			
I select the amount of detail to use, for the purpose of my writing.			

FEATURES OF WRITING	I can do this sometimes	I can usually do this	I need to improve this
I choose whether to write in a plain style or to include more detail and description for effect.			
I start sentences with a capital letter and end sentences with a full stop, question mark or exclamation mark.			
I write proper nouns with a capital letter.			
I select the correct verb tense to use and use it consistently.			
I vary the length of my sentences and write short sentences for effect.			
I start my sentences in different ways, to add variety and interest.			
I use a range of connectives to link my ideas together and to guide the reader through the text.			
I begin my paragraphs with a topic sentence.			
I develop the topic sentence by explaining in detail or by giving examples.			
I vary the position of subordinate clauses to make my sentences more interesting.			
I expand nouns and noun phrases, to add extra detail.			
I use imagery to help my reader to visualise the situation.			
I use repetition, contrasts, lists and patterning to add descriptive detail.			
I separate words, phrases and clauses in sentences with a single comma.			
I separate words, phrases and clauses in sentences with a pair of commas.			
I choose when to separate a subordinate clause from a main clause with a comma.			

FEATURES OF WRITING	I can do this sometimes	I can usually do this	I need to improve this
I select my vocabulary carefully so that my writing is as precise as possible.			
I use specialist vocabulary to suit my topic and reader.			
I learn the spellings and spelling patterns that I have trouble with so that I do not repeat the same mistakes.			
I check my drafts carefully so that I edit my work with the reader in mind.			

Now that you have reviewed your writing, record in your notebook the main things that you need to work on and improve. Keep checking your progress throughout the unit.

How do they do it?

A natural history text

David Attenborough is a famous natural historian who has produced a range of wildlife television documentaries and accompanying books. Below is an extract taken from *The Trials of Life*, the third and final volume in his award-winning *Life Trilogy*.

You may not immediately understand all the language used, because of the subject-specific terminology, but try to follow the gist of the passage. Remind yourself, too, of strategies for dealing with unfamiliar vocabulary, such as identifying the root of the word, breaking a word into syllables, and re-reading the sentence to see if the context helps you. If necessary, use a dictionary to support your understanding of particular terms used. Read the passage carefully several times, and then consider the points that follow.

There is one other way of communicating in darkness. Instead of signalling with sound, you can use light. The cold glow produced by luminous organisms has an eerie quality to us, since nearly all the light we create and experience is inextricably connected with heat. Animals, however, generate their light chemically. A complex protein called luciferin, when mixed with small quantities of an enzyme called luciferaze, will combine with oxygen and in the process give off a bright glow. Each luminescing organism has its own particular version of these compounds, but the reaction is a purely chemical one and it can be replicated in the laboratory with synthesised ingredients. Indeed, the dried bodies of small marine crustaceans that luminesce in life will glow brightly if they are simply moistened with water.

The commonest terrestrial luminaries are fireflies and glow-worms. They are neither flies nor worms but night-flying beetles, and they carry their light-producing chemicals in the hinder parts of their abdomen. Originally, they may have used their tiny torches simply to enable them to see where they were going. Many still do so. A female North American firefly, as she comes in to land, flashes her tail-lamp with increasing frequency until, just before touch-down, her flashes fuse into a continuous glow. As soon as she comes to a halt, she switches off entirely.

But these flashes are also used for signalling. The system is not unlike the Morse code as once used by naval signallers when working with hand-lamps, except that the fireflies' version is very much more complicated. Morse uses just two kinds of flash, one short and one long. Firefly flashes vary considerably in length, some lasting for as much as five seconds and others being repeated forty times within a single second at a speed so swift that our own eyes are unable to perceive the intervals between them. They also vary in the rate at which they are transmitted, the number of flashes in a sequence, the time between the signals and the pitches of intensity within the flash. All these variations have their significance.

World-wide, there are at least a hundred and thirty different species of firefly. The most spectacular are those that live in the mangrove swamps of South-east Asia. A journey in a canoe through certain creeks in Borneo and Malaysia at dusk may be uncomfortable because of persistent attacks from clouds of mosquitoes, but the reward is one of the most magical of all natural spectacles. As the sun sinks and dusk falls, scattered flashes begin to blink in the mangrove trees. Arcs of staccato lights, like the plumes of tiny fireworks, curve through the gloom as single beetles fly from one branch to another. Minute by minute, their numbers increase. Branches silhouetted against the sky become laced with tiny points of flashing green lights until the whole tree seems to sparkle and flicker. That sight itself is enough to take your breath away. But an even greater astonishment is to come.

Slowly the confusion of flashes begins to resolve itself into an order as the many thousands of insects synchronise their rhythms. Eventually, the whole tree, as a single unit, begins to pulse with light. Not all the mangrove trees are suitable for these displays. Many are inhabited by tree ants which will seize and kill any beetle that lands among them. So those trees that are illuminated often stand isolated above their rippling reflections with their pulsating lights outshining the stars that glitter in the black velvet sky behind them.

This is a fascinating text because it incorporates factual information and explanation as well as poetic description. In pairs or small groups, discuss the following features of David Attenborough's writing:

- Examine the **structure of each paragraph**. First, identify the **topic sentence** of each of the paragraphs. Next, identify the **purpose** of the remainder of the paragraph. For example, is it giving additional detail or information, giving examples, or providing an explanation?

- Look, too, at the **ways** in which the **paragraphs are connected**. How have the ideas been linked across paragraphs? What **connectives** have been used to do this? How else have ideas been linked? For example, is there **reference back** to previous points? Is there **repetition** of particular words or phrases? Do **pronouns** provide the cohesion?

- Consider the **sentence construction** used. Take note, particularly, of the way in which sentences begin:
    - Several sentences begin with **subordinate clauses**: *As soon as she comes to a halt, she switches off entirely* and *Instead of signalling with sound, you can use light.* (Note the placement of the comma, which serves to emphasise the subordinate clause.)
    - Several sentences begin with **adverbials**: *Indeed, the dried bodies of small marine crustaceans that luminesce in life will glow brightly if they are simply moistened with water* and *World-wide, there are at least a hundred and thirty different species of firefly.* (Note the comma placed after the adverbial, again for emphasis.)

- Find another example of each of the ways outlined above that David Attenborough uses to start his sentences. What is the effect of this varied sentence construction? Is there always a **comma** placed after an adverbial or an introductory subordinate clause? Consider, too, what happens to the commas when the subordinate clause is inserted into the middle of the sentence.

- Take note of the **variation in sentence length**. Although there are many long, complex sentences, these are mixed with short sentences, such as: *Many still do so.* What is the writer emphasising here with the shorter sentence? Look for other examples of relatively short sentences used in the extract. In each case, what is the writer emphasising with the varied sentence length?

- The passage **builds to a climax or crescendo**. Look at how David Attenborough moves from the more factual information and explanation given in the first three paragraphs of the extract, to the evocative description of the fireflies' display in the final two paragraphs.

  - Note the **emotive vocabulary** used in the final two paragraphs of the extract. **Adjectives** such as *spectacular* and *magical* are not ones you would usually associate with a natural history text such as this. Identify other examples from the final two paragraphs of vocabulary choices that are also emotive. What is the effect of this descriptive detail?

  - Note the **imagery** used to describe the fireflies' display: *Arcs of staccato lights, like the plumes of tiny fireworks, curve through the gloom* ... Discuss the image that comes to your mind when you read the figurative language used.

It's your turn

You are going to write your own natural history/scientific account that combines information, explanation and description, as in the example from Sir David Attenborough's work that you have just discussed.

Research a natural scientific phenomenon that interests you. You may choose any topic of interest, but possible subjects could be:

  - phosphorescence, as seen in the sea
  - autumn leaves – the changing colours
  - aurora borealis, or the Northern Lights
  - lightning.

As far as possible, it would be best to describe something you have managed to see for yourself, as part of the exercise is to write an accurate, yet evocative, description of the process. Thus, if you have not seen for yourself the subject of your preferred topic, try to watch a video or study a clip on CD-ROM as part of your research. This will help you to get across an accurate visual description.

Once you have researched your subject, write an account of it that **combines information, explanation** and **description**. The **purpose** is for your peers and teacher to gain a clear understanding of the process and for them to understand some of the beauty of the phenomenon. You should aim to write the information and explanation of the process first, in the first one to three paragraphs, and then to write the description, in the next one or two paragraphs (following the model of Attenborough's writing).

Try to use as many of the techniques that you have discussed that were used in the extract from *The Trials of Life*. Try, too, to address your targets from the introductory part of this unit. Once you have written your account, edit it carefully before asking your response partner to consider its effectiveness with you.

How do they do it?

Autobiographical writing

The next two extracts concern human survival. The first has been taken from Sir Ranulph Fiennes' autobiographical account of a journey around the earth, which took the explorers three years. This extract, taken from his account of the trip, *To the Ends of the Earth*, occurred towards the end of the second year of their expedition.

For three long days we plodded through deep snowfields with temperatures at −20 degrees. Because the exercise was unbroken we wore but two layers of clothing, as for walking in the Welsh hills, and only felt cold when we stopped for more than two minutes to drink or eat snow. The stillness was immense. No musk-oxen now. Nothing and no one.

On 23rd September we camped at the foot of the great Eugenie Glacier, its well-formed snout armed with layers of glistening teeth, stalagmites from a previous summer's brief melt. Mist rolled over the plateau from the east but now the very rim of the Grant Icecap brushed our left flank and, spurred on by the increasing cold, we limped at last to the northern tip of the plateau. There were many steep snowbanks to climb up or slither down. On one of these Charlie bruised his hip but, after a short rest, continued as before. In awe we laboured beneath the towering icefalls of Mount Wood where twin glaciers tumbled 2,000 feet down to a lonely lake. Here everything had a contorted temporary look, gigantic blocks of ice, scarred and smudged with alluvial muck and blackened walls of ice, reared up like monster waves frozen in the act of crashing against some puny dam. In the wary hush of this place where no birds sang, some new and cataclysmic upheaval seemed imminent. Crane your neck up to ease the pain of the sledge harness and the skyhigh icefalls appeared to teeter from their summits.

Thankful to leave, I sought a tiny stream outlet from the lake. Fingers of frost crept over the primordial environs of the lake and we stumbled by good luck into a corridor, some ten yards wide, between two boulder outcrops. This narrow rock-girt passage immediately descended, in curves and steps, to the west-north-west. There could be no doubt we were in the upper canyon of the Grant River, a winding ravine that falls for thirty miles to the sea. Once in it there was no further need to navigate, there being no branch-off valleys. The only place to camp was on the river ice. All game followed the river too and myriad little hoof prints of fox, hare, lemming, caribou and wolf, dented the snowdrifts all about.

The metal spikes of our snowshoes, long since blunted by rock and slate, no longer gripped the sheet-ice. Every few minutes evil language echoed off the narrow canyon walls as one or other of us slipped and crashed over onto the rocks. Often our snowshoes smashed through the ice and dropped two or three feet down to the streambed. Thanks to the snowshoes, awkward though they were, there were no sprained ankles.

In this extract, Ranulph Fiennes manages to effectively recreate both a sense of the effort involved in the group's travels and their awe at their surroundings. Note the following aspects of his writing which help to convey this:

- The precision of his **vocabulary** choices, particularly the **verbs** used to describe their movement, such as *plodded, limped* and *laboured*. What does this selection of verbs suggest to you about their journey? What other verbs can you find that convey the effort of the group and some of the difficulties they encountered?

- Look again at the last three sentences of the first paragraph, which are all very **short sentences**: *The stillness was immense. No musk-oxen now. Nothing and no one.* Only one of these sentences is actually a complete sentence; which one is it? What is missing from the other two sentences? What is the effect of using *Nothing and no one* to end the paragraph?

- The final two sentences in the first paragraph also contain **repetition** of *no* (echoed in the writer's choice of *nothing* as well). What is the effect of this?

- The passage contains some superb **imagery**. Work with a partner and each take one of the images from the second paragraph (the metaphor, or personification, describing Eugenie Glacier, or the personification and simile describing Mount Wood) and sketch what you visualise when you read the description of the geographical feature. Make your sketch/sketches as detailed as possible, then label the different parts, showing the aspects of the image that came into your mind when you read the description. Next, share your sketch with your partner, explaining your drawing. Discuss any differences in interpretation you may have had. You both need to ensure that you refer to the text closely in your discussion of the imagery. Now write a detailed comment, explaining how the imagery used by Fiennes influenced your sketch.

There are also other aspects of Ranulph Fiennes' writing that you could use as a model to help your writing to reach Level 6⁺. Take careful note of the following features which include some other characteristics of confident and able writers:

- Apart from the **verbs** already discussed, the **vocabulary** of the passage is incredibly effective. Re-read the passage to yourself, then select one of your favourite sentences. Try to identify why that particular sentence made an impact on you. What particular words or phrases stand out? What do they suggest? Why do they stand out? Discuss your ideas with a partner.

- What is the effect of the **alliteration** of *Fingers of frost*? Would the effect have been different if the alliteration had focused on a different sound? Try to give a reason for your answer.

- The author **expands noun phrases** to add to the detail of the passage. Consider the following sentence: *On 23rd September we camped at the foot of the great Eugenie Glacier, its well-formed snout <u>armed with layers of glistening teeth</u>, stalagmites <u>from a previous summer's brief melt</u>.*
  We will focus on two of the several noun phrases that have been expanded in this sentence. Firstly, look at the detail given about *the great Eugenie Glacier*: the expanded noun phrase is *its well-formed snout armed with layers of glistening teeth*. The *glistening teeth* in this part of the sentence have also been expanded in more detail, when the author continues *stalagmites from a previous summer's melt*. Why do you think authors expand noun phrases? What is gained by inserting extra detail into that one sentence instead of writing several sentences? Now find two or three other examples of where expanded noun phrases have been used. For each of these, explain the effect of including the additional information.

- Ranulph Fiennes creates a conversational **style** through the insertion of **drop-in clauses**, or additional information inserted into his description. For example, consider the following sentences:

  Thankful to leave, I sought a tiny stream outlet from the lake.

  Fingers of frost crept over the primordial environs of the lake and we stumbled by good luck into a corridor, some ten yards wide, between two boulder outcrops.

  Thanks to the snowshoes, awkward though they were, there were no sprained ankles.

  In each of the above examples, identify the additional information that has been inserted that helps to make the style more conversational. What do you notice in general about the punctuation of these extra pieces of information?

- Is there any other advice you would give a fellow pupil if trying to learn from Fiennes' examples? Look particularly at words and phrases such as *thankful, good luck, thanks*. What do these suggest about the writer's tone and character? What clues are there in these examples about his attitude?

The final extract has been taken from Beth Leonard's autobiographical account, *Following Seas*, in which she describes how she and her partner, Evans, sailed around the world in their thirty-seven foot sailboat, *Silk*. This account was written about their experience of a storm – and is describing the tenth day of sailing in such conditions.

As with the David Attenborough extract, there may be subject-specific vocabulary you do not understand. Don't worry about the precise meaning of every word for now; just read the passage carefully and try to get the gist of what's happening. Remember, too, to apply strategies for dealing with unfamiliar vocabulary.

August 4, 1994. I thought perhaps I would go mad.

I stood gripping the handrails on the companionway steps looking out through the clear plastic hatchboards at the chaos in the cockpit. The two port cushions lay half on and half off the cockpit seat. A snake's nest of tangled sheets writhed around on the cockpit sole with some rags and sponges caught in their coils. On every side, a claustrophobic horizon of jagged teeth surrounded us where the navy blue seas reared up against the sky. With a thunderous roar, yet another wave crashed into Silk's port side just aft of the beam. The wall of green water that engulfed the coachroof streamed over the hatchboards and showered through the sides of the companionway hatch, soaking my right shoulder and arm and spilling down my neck. Outside, water seethed over the coaming and half-filled the cockpit, floating cushions, line, and sponges.

The wave's slap skewed our stern to starboard and heeled Silk over hard to leeward. While my right arm and left leg tensed to keep me from falling down on the swinging stove below me, Silk's lee toerail submerged, and the rush of water along her starboard side sounded like the passing of a freight train. The stern being thrown off to leeward swung the bow the opposite way, and a mad clatter of halyards ensued as the wind whooshed around the mast and set them vibrating. With the change in wind angle, the plywood arm on the windvane flopped over to one side to correct Silk's course, and the wheel swung through half a revolution in response. After a long minute, the cockpit drained, Silk regained her proper heading, and I relaxed my stance on the stairs.

But my mind remained clenched like a fist.

After ten straight days of living in a front-loading washing machine, I wanted just ten minutes of peace. I wanted the wind to stop whistling in the rigging, the waves to stop crashing on the hull, the halyards to stop slapping the mast. I wanted to be able to walk across the boat without holding on to a handgrip, set something down and have it stay where I put it, cook without strapping myself in place, complete my morning workout without being thrown off the cockpit seat. I wanted to go out on deck without getting drenched, do a sail change upright instead of on my knees, and climb into my bunk without stripping off my salty clothes. I wanted to stay in that bunk without a lee cloth, sleep for more than ten minutes at a time, dream of anything except the heaving sea. I wanted to open up a single hatch or portlight and let the fresh air chase away the odour of stale bodies and mildewed bedding. In my head, I screamed at the ocean, railed at the waves, cursed Mother Nature herself. I pictured myself lying down on the cabin sole and giving vent to a temper tantrum worthy of the tempest all around. Instead, I stood gazing out through the hatchboards, impotent anger churning my stomach and knotting the muscles in my neck.

Halfway across the Indian Ocean and I wasn't sure how much more I could take. Worse, the most dangerous part of this ocean remained to be crossed. Off the eastern coast of

South Africa we would find ourselves in an ocean current that, in gale conditions, regularly raised seas that would dwarf those clawing at the sky all around us. Ahead of us waited the one stretch of ocean along our entire route that could duplicate the terrifying conditions we'd experienced in our first storm. In spite of the many miles we had sailed since, the thought of that storm still tensed my jaw against the remembered cacophony and filled my mouth with the coppery taste of my own fear. With each passing day, with each passing mile, we drew closer. But already I felt battered, beat up, and bruised by this sea.

Beth Leonard, the author, uses several techniques that are similar to those used by Ranulph Fiennes in the previous extract. As you have already had several attempts at analysing texts with structured support, you are going to do the first part of this exercise with a partner or group of your peers, but without the same level of direction that has been supplied previously.

 Examine the text closely, and look for ways in which the author effectively describes her experience. Remember, for every technique you identify, you need to examine its impact and effectiveness. To help you to focus your discussion, look particularly for the following features which have already been examined in the previous extract:

- the precision of the **vocabulary** selected
- the extensive use of **imagery**
- sound effects, such as **alliteration**
- **variation in sentence length**
- **repetition** of key ideas or phrases
- **expanded noun phrases**
- the **personal, conversational style** and **tone**
- any other techniques used that made an impression on you.

Apart from the features you have already discussed, you may also have noticed some or all of the strategies discussed below being used by the author. What's interesting is that several of these techniques will also be discussed in the unit on writing to argue, persuade and advise – another indication of the way in which the different text-types overlap.

● In addition to alliteration, the author also uses another sound effect, **onomatopoeia**, to good effect. For example, *the wave's <u>slap</u>, a mad <u>clatter</u> of halyards*, and *the wind <u>whooshed</u> around the mast . . .* Can you find other examples from the text? What is the effect of the onomatopoeia on the reader?

● The **structure of the paragraphs** is interesting too. Like Ranulph Fiennes, Beth Leonard also uses **short sentences** to add emphasis to parts of the text, and to slow the pace, but her short sentences stand on their own as short paragraphs. Why do you think she does this? How effective do you find the strategy?

● The author effectively uses **lists** in several sentences. Look again at this example:

> *I wanted the wind to stop whistling in the rigging, the waves to stop crashing on the hull, the halyards to stop slapping the mast. I wanted to be able to walk across the boat without holding onto a handgrip, set something down and have it stay where I put it, cook without strapping myself in place, complete my morning workout without being thrown off the cockpit seat.*

(A further three sentences begin with *I wanted . . .*) What is the effect of this cumulative listing technique? Can you think of other examples where you have seen this strategy being used?

● As well as the lists, the author also regularly uses a **pattern of three**. This is when three ideas are given together in one sentence or one paragraph. Advertisers have found odd numbers of points are easier to remember, and using three also gives the sentences a pattern or rhythm. Apart from all the sentences which begin *I wanted . . .*, here are two examples from the text: *In my head, I screamed at the ocean, railed at the waves, cursed Mother Nature herself* and *But already I felt battered, beat up, and bruised by this sea.* Why is this strategy effective? Once you become conscious of it, you will find that it is a common feature of several types of writing.

It's your turn

You are now going to write about a time when you were tested: a time when you faced a difficult situation or a challenge.

Firstly, think about the experiences you may have had when you have been frightened, when you have been responsible for your safety or the safety of others, or when you have faced an unknown situation. You may possibly have experienced some extreme weather conditions; you may have been on a trip that went wrong; you may have had to help someone who was injured. To help you to generate ideas, try a mind-mapping activity. Don't limit any options at this stage – just allow your ideas to spark off one another.

Once you have chosen your situation, shut your eyes and try to imagine yourself in that setting again. What happened? What could you hear, see, feel, smell, touch? When did you realise something was wrong? How did you know? What did you do? Who was with you? How were you feeling? What were the responses of the others? Generate another mind-map, this time focusing on the experience you will be writing about. Remember to use all your senses, to choose your vocabulary very carefully, and to think of appropriate imagery to convey your situation to the reader.

Plan your writing, including how you will link your paragraphs. Think about your sentence length and sentence construction. Where do you need shorter sentences to add emphasis or create tension? Where do you need to include extra information, in the form of subordinate clauses or expanded noun phrases?

Once you have planned your work carefully, revisit your targets for this unit on pages 31–33. What aspects of your writing do you particularly want to address in this piece of work?

Now write your descriptive account of a testing time you have experienced.

Revising your drafts

When you've finished your drafts, you need to work with a partner to revise them before you write final versions. Check over the following features:

- Is it **clear** what you have said? Ask your partner to read your drafts. Ask them to mark places where they aren't sure what you mean. Ask them to mark places where the sentences don't follow on clearly.
- Have you used a range of **descriptive techniques**? (For example, emotive language, imagery, repetition, giving extra detail in subordinate clauses or expanded noun phrases, using sound devices such as alliteration or onomatopoeia, using a variety of sentence length and sentence structures.)
- Have you thought about **verb tenses**? Check that they are consistent. If there is a change of tense, there should be a good reason.
- Are your **pronouns** clear? (Ask your partner to read your drafts, highlighting each pronoun. If they aren't sure what the pronoun refers back to, they should put a question mark in the margin. You'll then need to make it clear.)

And:

- Have you used a **single comma** to **mark off words and phrases** from the rest of the sentence and to separate items in a **list**?
- Have you used a **single comma** to separate **co-ordinate clauses** (beginning with *and/but/or*)?
- Have you separated some of your **subordinate clauses** from main clauses with **single commas**? (Remember the range of **subordinators** – for example, *because, since, as, so, so that, to, in order to, how, if, unless, although, instead of, who, why, which, that, how*.)
- Have you used a **pair of commas** to mark off words, phrases or even whole clauses, when they are dropped into the middle of sentences?
- Have you used a **range of punctuation**?

And:

- Have you used a range of sentence structures:
  - using **lists** or **repeated ideas**
  - starting a sentence with a **subordinate clause**
  - **dropping** a word, phrase or clause **into** another clause
  - using **short sentences** for emphasis.

And:

- Have you used a **topic sentence**, which you **develop** in the rest of the paragraph?

And finally:

- Check your draft carefully for the **spelling patterns** you know you have trouble with.

And you could try ...

- Choose a curriculum area and subject that interests you. Do some research on an extension topic (something that you have not studied in detail in class), with the aim of presenting the information to your teacher and peers. Once you have studied your chosen topic, write your information up clearly, with the aim of making your subject accessible and interesting to your audience.

- Find a subject in the newspapers or in the news on the television that is current, but about which you know very little. Research your subject in detail, with the purpose of explaining the context and background to your teacher and peers. You may want to include visual aids, such as diagrams or charts to help you to present your explanation to your audience.

- Write about a travel experience, focusing on presenting it in two different ways. For example, you could write about a day when you felt threatened while travelling, and then rewrite the event, focusing on changing the experience into a positive one.

- Do some further reading of travel writing or autobiographical writing. Read a range of authors to discover those whose style you enjoy. Now prepare a description of some of your chosen authors' work, to present to your peers. Your aim is to explain why you like their writing and to describe an extract that you particularly enjoyed. As an extension to this task, you could also try to write your own autobiographical account in the style of the author you have selected to study in detail.

- Think about a career you may wish to follow once you have left school. Research your chosen career, to help you to consider your choice more thoroughly. Your aim is to produce an information leaflet for GCSE students, outlining:
  - the examination or entry requirements
  - where you have to study and the subjects you will study
  - career progression
  - the working conditions and benefits, including salary scales
  - a topical issue involving the profession that interests you
  - a case study, explaining a typical day in the life of someone working in that career.

Unit Three

Writing to persuade, argue, advise

In this unit, you will:

- think about what is special about writing to persuade, argue, advise

- review your own writing, to see what needs to be done to make it a sound Level 6$^+$

- look at how a professional author writes a leaflet to persuade, argue, advise

- draft your own writing in this form.

Main National Framework Objectives Covered: 7Sn1, 7Sn8, 7Sn13a/d/e/, 7Sn15, 7Wr1, 7Wr15, 8Sn1, 8Sn6, 8Sn10, 8Wr2, 8Wr14, 9Sn3, 9Sn6, 9Sn7, 9Sn9, 9Wr14

Writing to persuade, argue, advise – what is it?

This kind of writing is very common both in and outside school. If we look at each aspect separately, we can see that:

- Writing to **persuade** should make readers see things from the writer's point of view. It uses emotive language to work on the reader's feelings. It repeats words (repetition) and may ask the reader rhetorical questions to make the writer's point strongly. It gives detailed examples to help readers understand what the writer means.

- Writing to **argue** should persuade a reader with a logical argument, signposting its structure with connective words and phrases. It persuades by giving reasons and detailed explanations. It also persuades by discussing opposite viewpoints. It then shows where these views are wrong.

- Writing to **advise** should make the reader want to follow the instructions given. It can persuade the reader by sounding friendly and informal. However, if the writing sounds formal, it can persuade because it seems important, speaking with authority.

In this unit, you will study a lengthy leaflet intended to persuade readers to contribute to charity. To help you think further about the features of this kind of writing, discuss the following text-types. Which ones are meant to persuade? Which ones are meant to argue or to advise? Sometimes, they may do more than one of these things, like the text you will study in this unit. Discuss the list and see what you think.

a science fiction novel
a private diary
a newspaper report on a volcanic explosion
a newspaper editorial
a novel set in the Middle Ages
an instruction manual for a video
a recipe for lasagne
an advertisement for a supermarket
an essay about 'Macbeth'
a cricketer's autobiography
a leaflet from Friends of the Earth

a letter from a friend who has moved away
a war story
an essay in History about the causes of World War One
a letter to your local council, complaining about the lack of safe routes for cyclists
a letter to a newspaper about vandalism
a report on an experiment in science
your favourite joke

What makes a good piece of writing to persuade, argue, advise?

You now have a general idea about what the range of writing to persuade, argue and advise is like. For homework, collect as many examples of these types of writing as you can. Look in newspapers and magazines. Look at recipes and instruction manuals. Collect leaflets from shops, local council offices, or tourist offices. Look through the writing you do at school. Look at writing in other subjects, as well as in English.

 Working in groups, look at the examples you have collected. Remember what you know about non-fiction text-types. What **features** of writing to persuade, argue and advise can you pick out? Do you think that some of your examples get their ideas across more clearly or more strongly than others? Can you explain why?

Look for:

- how the writer catches the reader's attention at the start
- the viewpoint chosen by the writer. Is it first person (*I/we*) or third person (*he/she/it/they*)?
- how the writer addresses (speaks to) the reader
- how informal (more like speech) or formal (more like writing) the voice of the writer sounds
- the persuasive techniques used by the writer. Look for emotive language, repetition, or rhetorical questions
- the main tense used by the writer
- any use of modal verbs (like *should, would, must*)
- any places where passive forms of verbs are used
- different sentence lengths and sentence patterns
- the range of connectives which the writer uses
- when the writer starts new paragraphs
- how the writer develops the topic sentence of paragraphs. Look for extra detail or examples.

As a class, make up a list of the features that you would expect to find in writing to persuade, argue and advise. Don't worry at this stage about how the features affect meaning. Just collect a list of features. You will see how these features are used, later in the unit.

 Record the list in your notebook. You might present what you have learnt as a wall display.

How can you improve your own writing?

Collect two or three pieces of your own writing to persuade, argue and advise. Talk to your partner. How many of the features do you use already? What features do you need to improve?

On this and the following pages, there are grids which show in detail the things you need to do for a sound Level 6+. There are a lot of things to think about, but don't worry. A lot of them you will already be doing well. Some, though, you will need to improve. The grids will help you think about which areas you need to improve. If you are not sure about a feature, your teacher will be able to explain. You could also wait to see how the feature is used later in the unit.

Copy the grids into your notebook. (It may also be possible for your teacher to photocopy them.) For each feature, put a tick in the box which applies to you. When you have finished, you will be able to see what aspects of your work you need to focus on in the rest of this unit. You will then be able to track your targets and improvements as you write.

FEATURES OF WRITING	I can do this sometimes	I can usually do this	I need to improve this
I capture the reader's interest with an effective heading or opening sentence.			
I know how to choose a personal (*I/we*) or impersonal (*he/she/it/they*) viewpoint.			
I make sure that it's clear what pronouns refer back to.			
I know when to speak to the reader in a formal or informal way.			
I have a clear idea of who the reader is, and how I want he or she to react.			
I choose formal or informal words where I need to.			
I use emotive language to persuade the reader.			
I use repetition to persuade the reader.			
I use rhetorical questions to persuade the reader.			

FEATURES OF WRITING	I can do this sometimes	I can usually do this	I need to improve this
I know when verbs are in the past or present tense.			
I don't vary verb tenses unless there is a good reason.			
I use a range of modal verbs, and I know about their effect.			
I use passive verbs, and I know about their effect on meaning.			
I end sentences with a full stop and start them with a capital letter.			
I write names with a capital letter.			
I write short sentences for emphasis.			
I begin sentences with subordinate clauses for emphasis or variety.			
I begin sentences with adverbial phrases for emphasis or variety.			
I drop words, phrases and clauses into sentences for emphasis or extra information.			
I separate words, phrases and clauses in sentences with a single comma.			
I separate words, phrases and clauses in sentences with a pair of commas.			
I choose when to separate a subordinate clause from a main clause with a comma.			
I use a range of connectives to begin subordinate clauses.			
I use a range of connectives to link sentences and paragraphs.			
I use logical connectives to structure an argument.			
I start a new paragraph to show a change in topic or viewpoint.			

FEATURES OF WRITING	I can do this sometimes	I can usually do this	I need to improve this
I start a new paragraph to show a change in time.			
I use a topic sentence for each paragraph.			
I develop the topic sentence by explaining in detail or by giving examples.			
I keep a list of the spellings and spelling patterns that I have trouble with.			
I check my drafts carefully for the spellings and spelling patterns I have trouble with.			

Now that you have reviewed your writing, record in your notebook the main things that you need to work on and improve. Keep checking your progress throughout the unit.

Writing to persuade, argue, advise: a charity leaflet

Charities are an important part of our society. Their work ranges from television appeals for Children in Need to the activities of environmental groups like Greenpeace or Friends of the Earth. In order to carry out the work they do, they need to raise money, because they rely on donations from the public. One way in which they raise money is by publishing leaflets which **persuade** readers to support the charity. The leaflet which you will study in this unit also **argues** in a logical way, to gain support from its readers. At the end of the leaflet, also, the writers **advise** readers about how to donate money and support the charity. This particular charity is called Médecins Sans Frontières (MSF). It is an international organisation, which provides medical help to people in areas hit by warfare or by natural disasters. Here is the front cover of their leaflet:

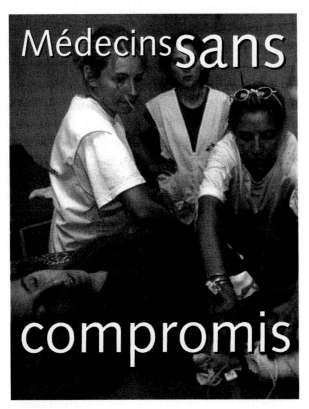

How do they do it?

- Use your knowledge of French to translate the name Médecins Sans Frontières (MSF). Also, translate the text on the front cover of the leaflet. What impression of MSF do you get from the name and from this text?

- Look, too, at the way this front cover makes a dramatic appeal to the audience. What expressions are shown on the faces of the figures in the picture? Look at the eyes, hands and arms of the figures. How do they help the dramatic effect?

- How would the picture and the text be persuasive to the audience? How might they fit the purpose of the leaflet?

It's your turn

- Your task, in the course of this unit, will be to write a leaflet, appealing for donations to a charity of your choice. The audience for the leaflet will be a general one, including adults. You will use the same techniques which the MSF writers use in their leaflet, and which you will study in this unit. You will need to decide on which charity you will write your own leaflet for. You will also need to collect factual information about your chosen charity, and to plan out your leaflet.

- Start by deciding for which charity you will write your leaflet. You could work in a small group, or on your own. You may have a clear idea already, or you may need to spend three or four minutes writing a list of all the charities and deserving causes you can think of. You might need to look through newspapers, or leaflets. Your charity could be for young or old people, for the environment, or perhaps it could be a local charity. Your school may already support charities or good causes, and you could write a leaflet for one of these organisations. Or you could even make up a charity of your own.

- You will need to collect plenty of information to use in your leaflet. Collect facts and statistics. Collect, too, any stories about events and people, which will add 'human interest' to your leaflet. Before you start looking for information, however, you need to find out what you already know about the charity or good cause. Spend five or ten minutes think-writing or mind-mapping, to get your ideas moving. Once you begin writing, it's surprising how much you can remember, because one idea reminds you of another thought.

- When you've collected what you already know about the charity or good cause, share your ideas with a partner. Can they add anything, or remind you of anything? Talk with your partner about what things you want to find out, and any questions you want to be answered. This will help you focus your research, when you look in libraries, or on the Internet.

- Finally, when you have collected your information and made notes, organise them using a mind-map or a paragraph plan. Aim to have a section on the background and aims of your charity, as well as between three and five sections about other aspects of what your charity does. What will be the main selling point for your appeal?

From its foundation in 1971, Médecins Sans Frontières has been a living, breathing, vital humanitarian presence in the world . . .

It was a group of exasperated French doctors who lit the spark which became Médecins Sans Frontières. Frustrated and angered at the inadequacies they saw in the global response to the Biafran Crisis in the Seventies, they were determined to create a unity of people – medical professionals and logistics experts – who, together, could bring humanitarian aid to whoever needed it, anywhere in the world.

And so Médecins Sans Frontières was born and with it a new vision and direction for the world's humanitarian response to crisis. Here at last was an organisation which really could cut through the barriers of bureaucracy to bring medical aid swiftly and effectively to the most vulnerable populations. What is more, here too was a new voice in the darkness, one free to speak out on the injustices it saw, to reveal the atrocities, to speak the truth and only that.

How do they do it?

- Here is the beginning of the MSF leaflet, in which the writers introduce the charity, its history and its unique appeal.
- Look first at the picture. What impression does it give of MSF?
- Now look at the main heading. Again, what impression does it give of MSF? Look in particular at the following features:
  - Starting the sentence with an **adverbial phrase**: *From its foundation in 1971*. This draws attention to the length of time MSF has been around. Note the comma after the adverbial, which also helps to emphasise the phrase. Note also the **associations** of *foundation*. Compare this word with, say, *beginning*, which the writers could have used. Look both words up in a dictionary. Why is *foundation* more persuasive? What impression does it give?

- Using a list of **emotive adjectives**, separated by commas, and intended to build up a persuasive picture of MSF. What impression of MSF does this list give?
- After the heading, we read the opening two paragraphs. The first paragraph **introduces** the historical background to the organisation. The second deals with the founding of MSF and **signals** to the reader **key ideas** which will be developed. With a partner, pick out from the second paragraph what you think will be the key words and phrases. Is the new paragraph started to show a **change of time**, a **change of topic**, or both?
- Note the following features:
  - The writing sounds **formal**. The sentences are often long, with **subordinate clauses** beginning with *who, which, that, where, when* and so on. The **vocabulary** is also formal, containing a lot of words which have three or more syllables. This makes the organisation sound to its audience as if it speaks with **authority**. Try replacing the longer words with simpler, shorter ones which mean the same. Does it make the writing sound less formal? Throughout the leaflet, make sure that you use the strategies you know for dealing with complex and unfamiliar vocabulary.
  - The verbs are in the **past tense**, because the writers are describing the history of MSF. The **pronouns** that go with the verbs are third person (*they/it*). The plural pronoun (*they*) refers to the doctors who created MSF. This third-person plural viewpoint gives the feeling of a team working together. The singular pronoun (*it*) could give an impersonal feeling, but the writers make the organisation seem almost alive. Can you find the words they choose which have that effect?
  - The paragraphs both begin with a **topic sentence**, which is then developed in greater detail. The smooth linking of sentences is helped by the use of **connective phrases** in the second paragraph. How many of those phrases can you pick out?
- Note also the variety of **sentence structures** that the writers use:
  - They use repeated patterns of phrases and sentence structures (*Here at last . . . here, too; swiftly and effectively; free to speak out . . ., to reveal . . ., to speak . . .*). What ideas do these repeated patterns emphasise? What impression do they give of MSF?
  - They sometimes begin sentences with extra information about the subject of the sentence, rather than beginning the sentence with the subject itself. For example:

    ***Frustrated and angered at the inadequacies they saw in the global response to the Biafran Crisis in the Seventies,** they (subject of main clause) were (verb) . . .*

    (Biafra: a country in Africa where there was a civil war and a serious famine.)

    This choice of word order emphasises the feelings of the doctors about what was going wrong. The technique is a little bit like the example you noted earlier, where the title starts with an adverbial phrase giving information about how long MSF has existed.
  - Another change of word order is to reverse the usual order of subject, verb and adverbial. Here, the adverbial comes before the verb and the subject comes after:

    ***Here at last** (adverbial) **was** (verb) **an organisation** (subject of clause), **which** . . .*

    This helps the writers to emphasise the fact that, finally, an effective organisation had arrived on the scene. Again, it's similar to the 'start with an adverbial' technique noted earlier.

It's your turn

So far, you have seen how the MSF writers make a dramatic appeal to the reader with the front cover of their leaflet. You have also seen how the writers introduce MSF and signal the key areas they are going to deal with, as well as looking at some of the techniques they use to persuade their audience. You have also gathered information and made notes about your own charity. You are now going to use those notes to write the beginning of your own leaflet.

- If you have not yet decided on a front cover, don't worry. Often, producing it at the end can be easier. Keep the text to a minimum, and make the images on the front dramatic. Your front cover should aim to persuade your audience to read further. You could cut images from newspapers and magazines, or you could import them using ICT. If you prefer, you could sketch the outline of the image you want, with detailed notes to show how an artist would develop your idea into a final version. (This is how commercial publishers would do it.)

- In writing your introduction, make sure that you try out the techniques used by the MSF writers, which have been pointed out earlier. First, write a detailed, descriptive **heading** of about four lines which sums up the impression you want to give of your charity. Begin the heading with an **adverbial phrase**. What do you want to emphasise with that phrase? Remember the comma, for emphasis. Include a **list** of **emotive adjectives**, to strengthen the impression you want to give of your charity. Don't forget the **commas** in the **list**.

- Give the **background** to your charity in the first paragraph. Think about how **formal** you want your writing to sound, and what vocabulary and sentence-structures will help that effect. Remember that you want your reader to feel that you have **authority**. In the second paragraph, signal the **key ideas** which you will develop in the following sections. Does your new paragraph change **time**, **topic**, or **viewpoint**?

- Check that you are writing in the **third person**, and that you use the **past tense** at least for the first paragraph. If you vary tense, make sure that there is a good reason.

- Think about **paragraph structure**. Start each paragraph with a **topic sentence**, which you then **develop** in greater detail. Remember to link sentences smoothly with **connective words** and **phrases**. You might find it useful to work with a partner and list all the connectives you can remember. Which ones would be right for these two paragraphs?

- Try out the range of sentence structures used by the MSF writers. For example, you could try **repeating patterns** of phrases and sentence structures. What ideas do you want to emphasise, with this repetition? What impression of your charity do they give? You could also try different ways of starting sentences:
  - Starting sentences with **adverbials**. This emphasises, for example, the time something happened, where it happened, or how it happened: *From its foundation in 1971, ...*
  - Starting sentences with **extra information about the subject**: *Frustrated and angry at the inadequacies ...* Again, what do you want to emphasise with this structure?
  - **Reversing the order** of subject – verb – adverbial for emphasis: *Here at last was an organisation ...*

The next section of the leaflet begins to develop the key ideas from the introduction. Discuss the meaning of the heading and sub-heading, and how they relate to the introduction. Remind yourself, also, of the strategies you use for dealing with complex or unfamiliar vocabulary. You'll find a lot in this section, because of the leaflet's purpose, and the audience it's aimed at.

sans
bureaucratie

But not without help.

Today, Médecins Sans Frontières is the world's largest independent international medical relief agency helping victims of armed conflict, epidemics, and natural or man-made disasters, in addition to others who lack health care due to geographical remoteness or ethnic marginalisation. Our objective is single-minded and determined at all times: to get access to and care for the most vulnerable, wherever and whoever they are.

To ensure that no-one stops us from achieving that objective, we have protected our freedom and independence with scrupulous care over the years. Our principles cannot be bought. We are in the pocket of no government, religious or economic power.

And there is one thing, and one thing alone, which keeps us that way. The support of private individuals committed to our cause.

In fact, we rely on discerning members of the public for the majority of our funding. Thanks to them, we are able to make no compromises to reach those who need us, when they need us.

Our work takes us to over 80 countries, worldwide, where the casualties of war, disaster and epidemic look to us to provide assistance. Each year about 2,500 doctors, nurses, logistics specialists and engineers of all nationalities leave on field assignments where, working closely with national staff, they conduct their own independent assessments, manage projects directly and monitor the impact of our aid. Through them, we also campaign locally and internationally for greater respect for humanitarian law and the right of civilians to impartial humanitarian assistance. We also campaign for fairer access to medicines and health care for the world's poorest and most vulnerable people. Treatable diseases, such as tuberculosis, meningitis and pneumonia, are still the leading causes of death in the developing world.

Above all, Médecins Sans Frontières is there when it needs to be for people who are in danger, people who are suffering, victimised or forgotten. Wherever they are, we are too.

How do they do it?

- Think first about the **purpose** of this section. It links with the introduction, picking up the idea of *cutting through the barriers of bureaucracy*, and it shows how MSF does this independently, without interference from governments or other organisations which might slow things down. Mentioning *no compromises* also picks up the idea of *sans compromis* from the front cover on page 53. For the first time, too, we come across the intended readers, whose support the writers argue for in this section. What impression does this section give of what MSF is like? How do the writers present the readers whose support they are asking for? What words and phrases do they use? Why would they be effective?

- Note the change of **tense** from the past to the present. Why do they do that? The **pronouns** have changed, as well, from a third-person viewpoint (*they/it*) to first-person plural (*we*). This makes the text more personal, in spite of the formal style. It gives the impression that MSF is a real team, with people working co-operatively together.

- Now look at the way the writers build up their **argument**.
  - **At the start of paragraphs**, they often use connective words and phrases as **signposts** for the reader. For example, *Today, And, In fact, Above all*. Readers get the impression that they are being taken through a logical structure, building up to the most important point which is signalled by *Above all*.
  - **Within paragraphs**, they **link** sentences with connective words and phrases such as *in addition* and *also*. They link sentences, too, by referring back to previous sentences (e.g. *that objective, Thanks to them, Through them*). They also link sentences by developing, explaining or giving examples of what the previous sentence has said. How many examples can you find of this?
  - Each paragraph has a **topic sentence**. The topic sentence is then developed in the sentences which follow, by giving examples or more detailed explanation. Choose two or three paragraphs, and discuss with a partner how each sentence links with the topic sentence. Does each paragraph change **topic**, **time** or **viewpoint**?
  - The paragraphs are **different lengths**, depending on the job they do. The first paragraph is quite lengthy, even though it has only two sentences. It introduces this section, telling readers what MSF does nowadays, and setting out its objectives. The next paragraph explains how MSF achieves its objectives, and how it is independent. The two paragraphs that follow are short, so that readers notice them. These paragraphs explain how MSF achieves its objectives and keeps its independence only because members of the public donate money. Then comes a long paragraph which gives examples of how the work of MSF reaches those who are in need. The final paragraph is a short one. Can you explain what job it does?

- Look also at the **sentence structure**.
  - You've already come across the technique of starting sentences with **adverbials**, and there are a number of examples in this section (e.g. *Each year . . ., Thanks to them . . ., or Through them . . .*). Apart from emphasis and variety, this technique helps to link sentences and paragraphs smoothly, as you've seen in the previous notes on building up the argument.
  - You've also come across the technique of **starting sentences with extra information** before the subject. There's one example, here:

    To ensure that no-one stops us from achieving that objective, we (subject of main clause) *have protected* (verb) *. . .*
    What impression do the writers want to give, by emphasising this information?

  - Another technique you've come across is **listing**. It can be used for emphasis, or to give a range of examples (e.g. *in the pocket of no government, religious or economic power* or *victims of armed conflict, epidemics, and natural or man-made disasters*). What other examples of listing can you find? A similar technique is **repeating patterns** of phrases or sentence structures (e.g. *to get access to and care for the most vulnerable, wherever and whoever they are.*). What other examples of repetition can you find? What ideas are they emphasising?
  - One new technique is **to start a sentence with a subordinate clause**. There is one example in this extract (<u>*Wherever*</u> *they are, we are too*). What idea do the writers want to emphasise, by starting the sentence in this way? Note also the single comma to separate the clauses.
  - Another new technique is to **drop a word, phrase or clause into another clause**. For example: *where, <u>working closely with national staff,</u> they conduct their own independent assessments . . .* Using this technique, writers can give and emphasise extra information. Note the pair of commas to mark off the 'dropped-in' phrase, here. What other examples of dropped-in words, phrases or clauses can you find?
  - Finally, although the MSF writers mainly use long sentences which have more than one clause, they occasionally use **short sentences** for emphasis. Can you find two or three examples of this technique? Can you explain what idea the writers are emphasising, in each case?

The section you have just studied comes from the middle of the leaflet. The MSF writers also include other sections, such as:

sans délai
But not without responsibility.

sans équipement
But not without professionalism.

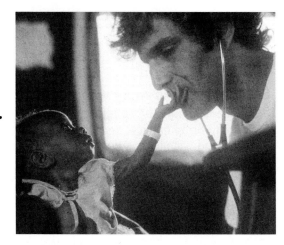

● Can you work out what the writers are trying to get across in these headings? What key ideas in the introduction on page 55 does each heading refer back to?

It's your turn

● Use your notes to draft out the middle sections of your leaflet. What sections will you need? How will they refer back to the key ideas in your introduction? How will you bring the reader in, during these sections?

● Remember the range of techniques that you need to include:
  ■ varying the **pronouns** from a third-person viewpoint (*they/it*) to first-person plural (*we*)
  ■ keeping the **tense** of verbs consistent. Don't change tense without a good reason.
  ■ using connective words and phrases as **signposts** for the reader, both at the start of paragraphs, and between sentences within paragraphs
  ■ making sure that the **topic sentence** is developed in the sentences which follow, by giving examples or more detailed explanation
  ■ using the **range of sentence structures** which you've studied so far in this unit
  ■ using **vocabulary** that makes you sound as if you speak with **authority**.

sans

excuses

But not without respect for the people we work to help.

We make no apologies for telling it and showing it like it is. As medical professionals we see it as our duty to bring medical assistance to populations in distress, and to speak out against injustices. As the world watched the horror of Kosovo unfolding in 1999, another, terribly brutal war was being waged in Sierra Leone. But, instead of focusing on the terrible plight of the civilian population and the atrocities being perpetrated against them, the news coverage was limited to the role of the UN forces in the conflict. Médecins Sans Frontières continued, and still continues to this day, to speak out against the brutality of the war and to demand from the parties involved free and impartial access to humanitarian assistance for the civilian population.

In the face of war, brutality and injustice, Médecins Sans Frontières maintains the freedom to operate without compromise, wherever we are needed, thanks to our supporters. Their donations keep us in the front line, bringing vital aid to those who need it, as well as giving us the independence to speak out if we have to.

If you would like to be a part of an organisation that is really making a difference in the world despite the best efforts of those with a very different agenda to stop it, then you can.

We ask for £10 a month. Not because that's a nice round figure to throw at you, but because medical aid does not come cheap.

£10 a month by banker's standing order can achieve a great deal over the course of a year. It can, for example, buy a basic Dispensary Kit containing drugs and medical equipment to serve a displaced population of 3,000 people for a whole month. Or it can provide a Surgical Kit containing 24 essential instruments for carrying out emergency operations in the field.

please tell us you're with us because

you we cannot do without

The one thing we cannot do without is support like yours. Particularly regular support – something each month by banker's order – because it means we can plan ahead confident that the funds we need will be there, and it means we don't have to waste money on administration which we could be spending on saving lives.

Giving by banker's order is easy for you too. No hassle. No time wasting. Just your money getting to where it's needed, fast.

There are several ways you can start supporting Médecins Sans Frontières today.

You can complete and return a banker's order instruction.

You can call free on 0800 731 6732 during office hours with your bank details.

Or go to www.uk.msf.org/access

However, and whatever, you decide to give, thank you.

We couldn't do what we do without people like you.

How do they do it?

- The text on the previous page is the last page of the MSF leaflet. Read through the *sans excuses* section, and consider its **purpose**. Discuss how it **relates back** to key ideas in the introduction on page 55. It does this to bring the leaflet to a conclusion, reaching the final stage of the **argument** which the writers are putting forward, to **persuade** readers that they should support MSF. Look, too, at:

  - The **emotive language** used. Pick out examples. What impression are the writers trying to give?
  - The **tenses** used (past and present). Can you spot where the tenses change? Can you explain why each tense is used, in that place?
  - The **pronouns**. The first-person plural viewpoint (*we*) is maintained, but for the first time the writers choose to speak to the reader as *you* (second person). What's the effect of having these two pronouns together in this section?
  - The **paragraphing**. Look at how the **topic sentences** are developed in each paragraph – how the following sentences refer back, explain, or give examples. Pick out the **signposts** which help readers follow the argument, and which link sentences or paragraphs. Comment on the **paragraph length**. What information do the long paragraphs deal with? What about the short paragraphs?
  - The **sentence structure**. Can you find examples of **starting sentences** with **adverbials** or **extra information** about the subject of the clause? Can you find examples of starting sentences with **subordinate clauses**? What about examples of **dropped-in** words, phrases or clauses? What about **lists**, or **repeated patterns**? (In all these techniques, notice if **commas** are used, or not.) Finally, can you find any **short sentences**? In each case, can you explain what ideas are being emphasised by these techniques?

- In this section, there is new one technique which has not been noted before. In the second paragraph, we find examples of passive verbs. For example:

Subject	Auxiliary Verb	Past Participle
a terribly brutal war	*was being*	*waged*
atrocities	*(were) being*	*perpetrated*
the news coverage	*was*	*limited*

What pattern can you spot, which tells you that a verb is in the passive voice? The effect of passive verbs is often to make events seem impersonal, as if no one person is responsible for what has happened. How does that effect contribute to the meaning in this section?

- Finally, look at the last section (*please tell us . . .*), where the writers **advise** the readers on the steps they can take to support MSF. What impression do the writers give of MSF in this section? What impression do they want to give of the reader? Identify particular words and phrases which give that impression.

● Note the way that the writers give **advice** to the reader. They don't use **command verbs**, as you would usually expect, except in one case. Can you find that example? Instead of using commands, the writers use the **modal verb** *can* (*you can start . . .; you can complete . . .*) How is the effect of this different from using a command verb? What impression does this give of the way in which the writers are speaking to the reader?

● How many of the persuasive techniques which you have studied in this unit can you find in the final section?

It's your turn

● Now bring your own leaflet to a conclusion.

● Check that you have included at least one example of each technique mentioned previously.
   ▪ Use **emotive language** to persuade the reader. Don't vary **tenses** without a good reason. Think about **pronouns**, especially the effect of a first-person plural viewpoint (*we*) and speaking to the reader as *you* (second person).
   ▪ Develop the **topic sentences** in each paragraph, with the following sentences referring back, explaining, or giving examples. Remember the **signposts** which help readers follow the argument, and which link sentences or paragraphs.

● Vary the **sentence structures**. Start sentences with **adverbials** or **extra information** about the subject of the clause, or with **subordinate clauses**. Use **dropped-in** words, phrases or clauses. What about **lists**, **repeated patterns**, and **short sentences**? (In all these techniques, think whether if **commas** are needed, or not.) Finally, try to include at least one **passive** verb. What pattern do they follow? What effect does a passive have?

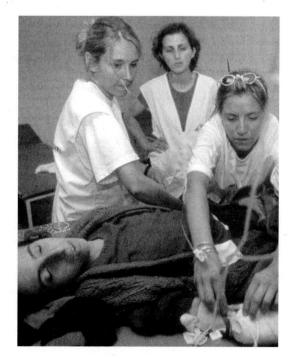

Revising your drafts

When you've finished your drafts, you need to work with a partner to revise them before you write a final version. Check over the following features:

- Is it **clear** what you have said? Ask your partner to read your drafts. Ask them to mark places where they aren't sure what you mean. Ask them to mark places where the sentences don't follow on clearly.
- Have you thought about **verb tenses**? Check that they are consistent. If there is a change of tense, there should be a good reason.
- Have you thought about **viewpoint**? (Third person if you want an impersonal effect, first-person plural to make your charity sound more friendly, like a team, and second person if you want to speak directly to the reader.)
- Have you used a range of **persuasive techniques**? (For example, emotive language, detailed examples, questions to the reader, using an authoritative voice, arguing using logical connectives, using a variety of sentence structures.)
- Are your **pronouns** clear? (Ask your partner to read your drafts, highlighting each pronoun. If they aren't sure what the pronoun refers back to, they should put a question mark in the margin. You'll then need to make it clear.)

And:
- Have you ended each sentence with a **full stop**? (Count the number of sentences you have written in each paragraph. Write the number in the margin. Then count the number of full stops. The numbers should be the same!)
- Do all your sentences **begin with a capital letter** and have you used **capital letters for names**? (Underline each sentence beginning and each name in what you have written. Is each first letter a capital?)

And:
- Have you used a **single comma to mark off words and phrases** from the rest of the sentence and to separate items in a list?
- Have you used a **single comma to separate co-ordinate clauses** (beginning with *and/but/or*)?
- Have you separated some of your **subordinate clauses** from main clauses with **single commas**? (Remember the range of **subordinators** – for example, *because, since, as, so, so that, in order to, how, if, unless, although, instead of, who, why, which, that, how.*)
- Have you used a **pair of commas** to mark off words, phrases or even whole clauses, when they are dropped into the middle of sentences?

And:
- Have you used a **range of connective words and phrases**? (For example: *first, second, to begin with, furthermore, next, all in all, to conclude, to sum up, overall, altogether; in other words, for instance, for example; therefore, consequently, as a result; otherwise, in that case, rather, on the other hand, alternatively, instead, however.*)

And:

- Have you used a range of **sentence structures**:
  - using **lists** (*a living, breathing, vital humanitarian presence*) or **repeated patterns** (*Here at last . . . here, too*)
  - beginning sentences with **extra information about the subject** of the sentence, rather than beginning the sentence with the subject itself (*Frustrated and angered at the inadequacies they saw in the global response to the Biafran Crisis in the Seventies, they* (subject of main clause) *were* (verb) . . .)
  - **reversing** the usual order of subject, verb and adverbial (*Here at last* (adverbial) *was* (verb) *an organisation* (subject of clause), *which* . . .)
  - starting a sentence with a **subordinate clause** (*Wherever they are, we are too*)
  - **dropping a word, phrase or clause** into another clause (. . . *where, working closely with national staff, they conduct their own independent assessments* . . .)
  - using **short sentences** for emphasis
  - using **passive verbs** to give an impersonal feeling.

And:

- Have you used a **topic sentence**, which you **develop** in the rest of the paragraph? (Mark with *Explain* or *Example* the sentences which follow the topic sentence. This will help you see how each sentence develops the topic of the paragraph.)

And finally:

- Check your draft carefully for the **spelling patterns** you know you have trouble with. (Use your spelling list to remind you.)

When you are ready, review your progress using the grids from pages 50–52. What features of writing have you improved? The more improvements you have made, the closer you are to a sound Level 6+.

And you could try . . .

- Collect a range of sentence structures from the examples of texts you put together at the beginning of this unit. Classify them into the different types of structures you now know about. Produce a wall display, showing the different types of structures. Try to make your examples big enough to read from a distance, so that your display will be useful for people who use the classroom.

- Work with a group of people from your class to run a campaign. Your campaign could be about local issues, such as safer roads or improving things for young people to do in the area. Or it could be about organising a major event such as a rock festival. Whatever you decide, you have opportunities to produce a range of writing to persuade, argue, advise – for example adverts, letters to newspapers, opinion articles, editorials, publicity leaflets. There are opportunities, also, for a range of opinions and viewpoints on your campaign, some of which you will have to argue against logically, to make your own viewpoint more persuasive.

Unit Four

Writing to analyse, review, comment

In this unit, you will:

- **think about what is special about writing to analyse, review, comment**

- **review your own writing, to see what needs to be done to make it a sound Level 6[+]**

- **look at how successful writers analyse, review, comment on texts**

- **draft your own writing in this form.**

Main National Framework Objectives Covered: 8Sn1, 8Sn2, 8Sn5, 9Sn1, 9Sn2, 9Sn3, 9Sn4, 9Wr16, 9Wr17

Writing to analyse, review, comment – what is it?

When you write to **analyse**, **review** and **comment**, you might be writing about a very wide range of things. The thing you might be writing about is called the **subject matter**. The subject matter might be anything from a new novel, a poem or book of poetry to a sports event, like the England football team's progress in the World Cup or an historical event, like the Battle of Hastings. It might be about an issue like whether Great Britain should join the Single European Currency.

A lot of the writing you do at school in English, in class or in examinations, is writing that asks you to analyse, review and comment. For your examinations at the end of Key Stage 3, you may have to read a text and then answer a question that asks you to analyse how a writer makes the reader feel sympathy for a character, or how a writer creates a tense, exciting atmosphere. For your GCSEs you may need to analyse a range of non-fiction materials, writing about the distinctive features of each, or about their purpose and how they achieve that purpose.

If you write like this for an examination, it is possible that a lot of the marks will be given for the level of your understanding of the text you are writing about, not for your ability as a writer. However, it is still very important to be able to write well about the text. The better you can express your ideas and use language powerfully and effectively to communicate your opinions and to show off your understanding of the text, the better your answer, and therefore your grade, will be.

Whatever the subject matter is, this kind of writing has three main features.

- The writing **reviews** the subject matter. This means the writing will 'look over', or 're-view' the whole text, having something to say about each part of it. It will explain each point so that the reader can understand what is being said, even if he or she has not actually read the text him or herself.
- The writing will **analyse** the subject matter. This means being clear about how to decide how good, effective or successful a text is, and then picking the text apart to see what the writer is doing, and how they are doing it. Different sorts of writing have different sorts of features. When analysing, you are writing about how well the writer has used the features found in that particular sort of text. If it is an extract from a story, it may be looking at the way the writer has described the setting, or the character's thoughts and feelings. If it is an advert, it may be looking at the writer's use of presentation features or persuasive language.
- The writing will **comment** on the subject matter. This means the writer will explore his or her own opinions about the text, using evidence, often as quotations, to back up and develop his or her ideas.

When writing to **analyse**, **review** and **comment**, the writer always has to remember what the reader wants to know. When writing for an examination, this is particularly important. The reader will be the marker, who will give a certain grade or level depending on how well the writer has written about certain things. The writer must be clear about what the reader wants to see, in order to give the student a particular level or grade.

Discuss the following text-types. Which ones are meant to analyse, review and comment? Discuss the list and see what you think.

a science fiction novel

a private diary

a scientific report on a new drug to fight flu

a newspaper comment on the Government's plans for the Railways

a novel set in the Middle Ages

an instruction manual for a video

a recipe for lasagne

a magazine article about three new cookery books

an advertisement for a supermarket

a report on two supermarkets' own brand chocolate bars

an essay about the Harry Potter books

a cricketer's autobiography

a leaflet from Friends of the Earth on the effects of building new nuclear power stations

an answer to a question about how a writer makes a story exciting

a letter from a friend who has moved away

a speech by a politician on how schools can be made better

an essay in history about the Battle of Hastings

a letter to your local council, complaining about the lack of safe routes for cyclists

a letter to a newspaper about vandalism

a report on an experiment in science

your favourite joke

a page in a teenage magazine about new films and videos

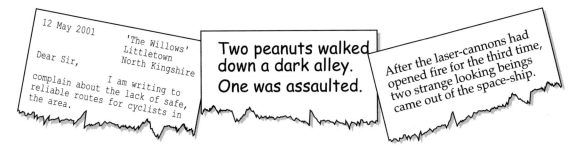

What makes a good piece of writing to analyse, review, comment?

You now have an idea about what writing to analyse, review and comment is like. For homework, collect as many examples of these types of writing as you can. Look in newspapers and magazines. Look at textbooks. Look on the Internet. Look through the writing you do at school. Look at writing in other subjects, as well as in English.

Working in groups, look at the examples you have collected. Draw on your knowledge of non-fiction text-types. What **features** of writing to analyse, review and comment can you pick out? Do you think that some of your examples are better than others at getting their ideas across to their audience? Can you explain why?

Look for:

- how the writer explains the text so that the reader can understand it
- how the writer organises his or her ideas into effective paragraphs
- how informal (more like speech) or formal (more like writing) the voice of the writer sounds
- how effectively the writer has developed ideas or linked one idea to another
- how many examples or quotations the writer uses
- how the writer comments on the quotations or uses them to explore or develop his or her ideas
- how the writer picks out the distinctive features of the text and writes about them
- how the writer gives his or her own opinion on the subject matter
- the variety of ways the writer starts sentences
- the use of subordinate and co-ordinate clauses
- the range of connectives that the writer uses
- whether the writer uses the passive voice for effect
- clear use of topic sentences by the writer.

As a class, make up a list of the features that you would expect to find in writing to analyse, review and comment. Record the list in your notebook. You might present what you have learnt as a wall display.

How can you improve your own writing?

Collect two or three pieces of your own writing to analyse, review and comment. Talk to your partner about the features you have been discussing. Some things you will be doing already. What things do you need to improve?

On this and the following page, there are grids which show in detail the things you need to do for a sound Level 6⁺. There are a lot of things to think about, but don't worry. A lot of them you will already be good at, but some you will need to improve. The grids will help you think about them. If you are not sure about a feature, your teacher will be able to explain. You could also wait to see how the feature is used during the unit.

 Copy the grids into your notebook. (It may also be possible for your teacher to photocopy them.) For each feature, put a tick in the box which applies to you. When you have finished, you will be able to see what you need to focus on in the rest of this unit. You will then be able to track your targets and improvements as you write.

FEATURES OF WRITING	I can do this sometimes	I can usually do this	I need to improve this
I know how to write in a formal style.			
I use appropriate vocabulary for a formal essay, analysing a text.			
I know how to summarise the text.			
I select particular features of different sorts of texts to analyse.			
I use carefully selected quotations to back up my ideas.			
I can insert quotations into sentences.			
I know how to explore ideas from words or phrases in a text.			
I separate words, phrases and clauses in sentences with a single comma.			
I separate words, phrases and clauses in sentences with a pair of commas.			
I choose when to separate a subordinate clause from a main clause with a comma.			

FEATURES OF WRITING	I can do this sometimes	I can usually do this	I need to improve this
I use a range of connectives to begin subordinate clauses.			
I vary the way I start my sentences.			
I use a range of connectives to link sentences and paragraphs.			
I start a new paragraph to show a change in topic, time or viewpoint.			
I link each paragraph to the next clearly, using connectives, pronouns, or references to earlier points.			
I use a topic sentence for each paragraph.			
I develop the topic sentence by explaining in detail or by giving examples.			
I use the passive for effect.			
I use a variety of words and phrases to link my paragraphs.			

 Now that you have reviewed your writing, record in your notebook the main things that you need to work on and improve. Keep checking your progress throughout the unit.

Writing to analyse, review, comment: analysing and commenting on an extract

You can analyse, review and comment on any piece of writing, whether it is a whole long novel or a short poem. Whatever the text, the skills you need are the same. You need to review the text, which means telling the reader enough about the text so that they can understand it. You need to analyse the text, identifying the distinctive features of a text and writing about them, in particular, writing about their effect on the reader. You need to use lots of quotations to back up your ideas, and you need to use the quotations as a springboard to comment on the text, which means developing and exploring your ideas about the text in detail.

In this unit, you will be focusing on writing the sorts of texts that you will have to do for your examinations at the end of Year 9 and for your GCSEs. For this sort of writing, you are often asked to read and analyse a short piece of writing or an extract from a longer piece of writing.

Looking at an analysis of a text

The following piece of writing was written by a student who was asked to read a passage about two men trying to cope with a disaster in a hot-air balloon, and then answer this question:

In what ways does the writer try to build up excitement and suspense throughout this passage?

The piece was written in exam conditions, which meant they did not have much time to plan or rewrite their work.

The writer tries to build up the feeling of excitement and suspense throughout this passage. At the start we are drawn straight into the story by the opening line 'two men hastily considered their difficult situation' we are immediately told something horrible is happening and want to know what. The author then increases the feeling of horror by telling us what might happen 'they could be swept miles of the coast'. The writer then tells us what they're going to do, showing how well they must know it but also go through what might happen if they do not do it; 'it would either drag it uncontrollably …' The phrase a bit later 'almost certainly drowned them' shows us the possibility of what might happen if something went wrong. The writer ends the first passage with a glimmer of hope 'leaving the capsule to float safely', but we are still left with the feeling of uncertainty, and want to know whether they will make it.

The way the writer describes Branson's thoughts and actions later in the passage adds to the suspense. We feel that we are actually there with him facing his questions. The writer does this by setting out this part of the passage as if he were thinking, throwing ideas about in his mind, and asking questions; 'was this going to be it'. The suspense is added to immediately by the writer telling us 'Branson believed he was about to die'. This makes us feel emotionally towards him, not wanting this to happen. Branson going back into the capsule and writing on the note 'I love you', moves us even more to how real this is to him. The writer increases the tension in the next paragraph (lines 46–50) by using a lot of simple sentences one after another, showing the sense of panic. He has not got time to think straight. The writer then starts to make Branson think about all the disadvantages of every option; 'he would drown', showing what little hope he thinks he has. He then throws in a bit of hope 'then they would both be safe', but we can still see there is not much hope left for him.

The mood of the last paragraph is an increasing feeling of hope. The author shows us this by making Branson see rescuers; 'Branson could see a ship – a Navy ship', we get the feeling that Branson knows he is going to be alright 'everything according to procedure'. By adding the feeling of coming out of a cloud into sunlight, 'it was clear' shows us the new hope in another way. The writer ends the passage again with the feeling of uncertainty again but with added hope 'and jumped'.

How do they do it?

- First of all, notice how the writer is confident in straight away **answering the question**. The writer knows what the reader needs to know and has used the first sentence immediately to focus on the question he has been asked to answer.
- His ideas are clearly organised into **paragraphs** and each paragraph focuses on a **different topic**. Each paragraph is effectively opened with a **clear topic sentence**. For example: *The way the writer describes Branson's thoughts and actions . . . adds to the suspense.* This sentence tells us that the writer is next going to analyse the description of Branson's thoughts and actions.
- The writer is also very good at **developing ideas**. In the first paragraph the writer explains how we are drawn into the story. He then explains how the author increases *the feeling of horror*.
- The writer is also successful at **linking ideas together**. For example, in the first paragraph, he mentions the sense of uncertainty in the text and then comes back to this idea later in the same paragraph.
- The writer uses **quotations** throughout his answer. He has 're-viewed' the whole passage by discussing many of its important sentences or phrases. He puts speech marks around quotations. Importantly, he has nearly always commented on the quotation. For example, he quotes: *two men hastily considered their difficult situation.* And then says: *We are immediately told something horrible is happening and want to know what.* He explains to us the effect of that quotation on the reader.
- Notice how the writer switches from **starting sentences** with *the writer* to using the third-person pronoun *we*; see the beginning of the second paragraph for an example. In this way, the writer alternates between exploring what the author of the text is doing, with discussing the effect of aspects of the text on us as readers.

- The writer uses *we* not *I*. This is good in a piece of writing like this because it helps create a **formal style**. He shows that his response as a reader is probably the response most people would have. Using *I* would have made the response seem too personal, the opinions of just one person. A review has to try and understand the responses other people might have, as well as expressing the writer's own views.

- The writer uses a wide variety of **sentence structures**. He is confident at using **subordinate clauses** in different places in the sentence. For example, here he places them in the **middle** and at the **end of the sentence**: *The writer then tells us what they're going to do, showing how well they must know it, but also go through what might happen if they do not do it* . . . He also can start sentences with a subordinate clause. For example: *By adding the feeling of coming out of a cloud into sunlight, 'it was clear', shows us the new hope in another way.* In addition, in this sentence, he has inserted the quotation *'it was clear'* as a **drop-in clause**. He uses a variety of **connectives** to start clauses or link them together: *and, but, as, by*, but often starts a clause with a word ending in –ing: *showing the sense of panic* or *facing his questions*.

- The writer uses the **passive voice** effectively. For example: *The suspense is added to immediately by the writer telling us Branson believed he was about to die.* The active would be *the writer adds suspense*. By using the passive, the writer puts the emphasis of the sentence onto the suspense which is the main focus of the sentence.

- The writer uses the full range of **punctuation** effectively. Commas are used singularly and in pairs to separate clauses. He uses semi-colons to introduce quotations. For example: *The author shows us this by making Branson see rescuers; 'Branson could see a ship . . .'*

- The writer uses **appropriate vocabulary** for a piece of writing like this. Words like *suspense, mood, excitement*, all keep the text focused on answering the question effectively.

- The combination of using the pronoun *we*, appropriate vocabulary, lots of quotations and a varied sentence structure all contribute to creating a **formal style** to this piece of writing. If you are writing to answer an exam question, you should write in a formal style. You should avoid slang or words that make your writing sound informal. When you include personal comment it is good to write with *I think* . . ., but when you are writing about the effect on the reader often it sounds more formal to write with *we* not *I*.

- Even though this writer is very competent and has written a very good answer there are some small mistakes. For example, he possibly should have started a new paragraph in the second paragraph, where he says *the writer increases the tension . . .*, because at this point he is writing about the use of simple sentences, which is a new topic and, therefore, needs a new paragraph.

It's your turn

You are going to write an analysis of a short text or extract from a text, using the same skills you have just read about. You are going to analyse how the writer makes the extract exciting or tense for us as readers. First of all, you need to find a suitable text to write about. A good place to look is from a short story, novel or autobiography you have been reading. Find an extract where the writer has made it exciting or tense. Make sure the extract is not more than two or three pages long.

Gathering ideas: making notes

Read the extract through two or three times until you are very familiar with the extract. Then make notes to answer these questions:

- What is the **main action** in the extract?
- Who are the **main characters** and what is the relationship between them?
- Has the writer described the **characters' thoughts** or **feelings**?
- Has the writer described any small **actions** or **gestures** by the characters that help you know what they are thinking or feeling?
- What has the writer described about the **setting** for the action? Are there any **details** he or she has included about the setting which help create a tense or exciting atmosphere, for example, about the weather or time of day?
- Has the writer used **imagery** to describe the setting or any of the characters? If so, what pictures are created in your mind?
- Has the writer included any **noises** in the background or **objects** that have scary or exciting associations?
- What **words** have been chosen to give you **pictures** of the action, or to fill out the characters' thoughts or feelings? Look especially at the choice of **verbs**. When has the writer used a verb that creates a clear picture of what is happening and when could he or she have used a less descriptive word? Look at the choice of **adjectives**. Where has the writer added adjectives to create noun phrases that give you more detail about objects being described?
- What **range of sentences** has the writer used for effect? Has the writer used short sentences to stop the reader, to make you pause on the moment being described? Has the writer used long sentences with lots of **co-ordinate clauses** to make the action seem breathless and fast?
- Has the writer used **paragraphing** to focus on a single, important event?
- Has the writer used **dialogue** to give you further information about the relationship of the characters or their thoughts or feelings?
- Are there any changes in the **tension** in the extract? Does it begin calm and then build up to a climax? Or does it die away at the end?
- What **questions** does the writer make you ask at the beginning of the extract that make you want to read on, to answer the questions?
- Has the passage been written in a **particular style**, or with an accent? Does that add to the atmosphere at all?
- Has the writer used the **passive voice** to emphasise particular events?

Gathering ideas: finding quotes

Once you have answered all these questions, you will have lots of ideas to write about to analyse the passage. You next need to decide which sentences, phrases or individual words you are going to use as quotations. If you have a photocopy of the extract, underline about ten to fifteen words, phrases or sentences you can use as quotations to back up your ideas. You might underline a piece of description, something someone says, an example of a short sentence, an action that gives clues to a character's thoughts or feelings? Double underline individual words or very short phrases that give you the most information, or create the fullest picture. You will use these words in particular to develop or explore your comments in detail.

Practising using the passive voice

One of the features of writing that is at Level 6+ is the use of the passive voice. Look at these two sentences:

The writer also creates suspense by describing the character's face in detail.

Suspense is also created by the detailed description of the character's face.

What is the difference in the way these two sentences have been written? The first sentence is in the **active voice**, with *the writer* at the beginning of the sentence and the second is in the **passive voice**, with *suspense* at the beginning of the sentence. Using a passive can have two main benefits. Using a passive means *suspense* is put at the beginning of the sentence. This can help focus our attention onto the fact that the sentence is about suspense and how it is created. Secondly, if you mainly write in the active, as most writers do, using a passive breaks this pattern, introducing variety into your sentence structure, so making your writing more interesting. You will not be expected to use the passive a lot in your writing, but it is a useful technique to have.

Practise using the passive by turning these **active** sentences into **passives**. The first one is done for you.

The writer <u>describes</u> the weather as warm and calm. (<u>active</u>)

The weather <u>is described</u> as warm and calm. (<u>passive</u>)

Before writing out the next sentences, ask yourself; which word will you have to put at the **beginning of the sentence** to write it in the **passive**? How will you have to change the **verb** when changing it from **active** to **passive**?

The writer shows the reader that George is the leader of the two men.

The writer gives us a detailed picture of the setting for the story.

The author creates an atmosphere of tension with the description of the clenched fist and narrowed eyes.

Steinbeck draws the reader into the story by his portrayal of this strange relationship.

Using appropriate vocabulary to create a formal style

You need to write in a formal style. This means, as you already know, using appropriate vocabulary in your writing. Here are some verbs that are useful in creating the right kind of style, particularly when discussing the effect of quotations on the reader:

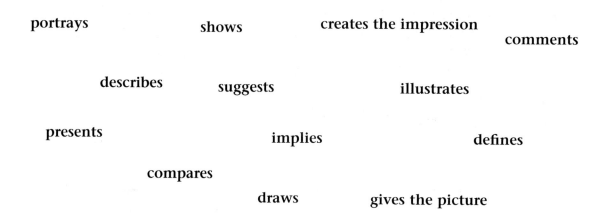

portrays

shows

creates the impression

comments

describes

suggests

illustrates

presents

implies

defines

compares

draws

gives the picture

Which of these do you use already? Are there any that you are not sure how to use? If so, ask a partner or your teacher for examples of how to use them.

Experiment at using these words in sentences so that you are comfortable using them when writing to analyse any kind of text. For most of these words you will need to start your sentence with *the writer* or *the author*. For example, *The author gives us a picture of* ... Equally, most of them can be used in the passive, if you start your sentence with *the reader*, or *we*: *We are given a picture of* ... If you use a mixture of both, it will ensure that you have a balance of comment on what the writer is doing and on how the reader is responding. It will also ensure a varied sentence structure, which is important for Level 6+.

Writing in detail

One of the most important skills you need in order to attain the higher levels at Key Stage 3 or grades at GCSE is the ability to write in detail. This is at the heart of what it means to analyse. You need to explore your ideas, so that you are turning them over, picking out different aspects of them. You need to develop each point, comparing it to another point or linking it to something you said earlier. Before you draft your writing about the text you have been gathering notes on, look at another example of writing to analyse, review and comment.

How do they do it?

This example is a paragraph from a piece of GCSE coursework by a student, comparing the opening chapters of two novels. In this paragraph, she is writing about the two main characters in *Of Mice and Men* by John Steinbeck.

I don't think that Lennie likes to see George angry and this relates back to the father/son relationship from earlier. 'Lennie looked timidly over to him. "George" ', it's like when a parent is angry, the child doesn't want to be in the way. The word 'timidly' gives the sense that he doesn't really want to ask, but has to. When Lennie asks "Where we goin' George?", Steinbeck writes 'The little man jerked down the brim of his hat and scowled over at Lennie.' I think that Steinbeck deliberately used the words 'little man' to show that even though Lennie is so huge and strong, George can intimidate and scare him.

- In this example, the writer gives a **clear topic sentence** that shows us that she is writing about one aspect of the father/son relationship of George and Lennie.
- She then gives a **quotation** and then **comments** on the quotation.
- By **commenting on a single word**, *timidly*, she begins to explore in more detail the nature of Lennie's feelings about George.
- She **develops** her idea by giving another quotation and then commenting on it.
- For a second time, she identifies and focuses on the **key words** that enable her to explore the idea further.
- In this paragraph she uses *I think* instead of *we* or *the reader*. This is appropriate here, because she is developing her own ideas about the text, rather than identifying a response that we would expect most readers to have.
- She uses a **range** of different **sentence structures**. In the first sentence, she uses two co-ordinate clauses joined together with the connective *and*. Later, she starts her sentence with a subordinate clause with the connective *when*.

Work out with a partner what the key is to exploring in detail and developing your ideas to the full.

- Always add a comment after a quotation, to explain how the quotation backs up the point you made.
- If possible, pick out a single word or very short phrase and use that as a launch pad to write in more detail about the point you have just made.
- Find another quotation that makes a similar point. Copy that and then comment on it, picking out the most interesting word or words in it and writing about them.
- Link this comment back to the original point you made at the beginning of the paragraph.

Here are some phrases that will help you write in the appropriate style when exploring in detail and developing your ideas in full.

The writer says . . .
The poet describes . . .
Next, he explains, . . .
Some people might say . . . but I think . . .
When he says . . ., I think it shows . . .
The phrase . . . could mean . . ., but on the other hand, . . .
Although . . .
This suggests to me . . .
I think the writer is showing us that . . .
The word . . . gives me a picture of . . .
The phrase . . . makes me think . . .
This is similar to when . . .
Another time when . . .
He also says . . .
This links back to . . .
In the same way . . .
You could say . . .
It is like . . .
Not only does he . . . but he also . . .
She is both . . . and . . .
Generally,. . . but here . . .
This makes us wonder . . .
On the one hand, . . . but on the other . . .

Experiment with these so that you can use them confidently and fluently.

Writing your analysis

Your task is to write an analysis that answers this question:

How does the writer make this extract interesting or tense for the reader?

You can write your answer in two ways. Either use the bullet points from the section on gathering ideas (see page 80) as a paragraph plan, and write about each bullet point separately one by one, or write about the text in the order that you read it. In other words, first of all write about the first one or two paragraphs. Then write about the next two or three paragraphs and so on.

You might like to try and experiment with both ways to see which you find most helpful for organising your ideas.

Whichever way you choose, you need to have a paragraph plan, which includes the main points in each paragraph and the main quotes you intend to write about.

Your paragraph plan might look like this:

description of setting	two or three ideas and quotes, with discussion of the quotes
description of character	two or three ideas and quotes, with discussion of quotes
vocabulary chosen for effect	two or three ideas and quotes, with discussion of quotes
use of dialogue	two or three ideas and quotes, with discussion of quotes
variety of sentence length	two or three ideas and quotes, with discussion of quotes

. . . and so on.

Or it might look like this:

lines 1–12	main ideas and quotes, with discussion of quotes
lines 13–24	main ideas and quotes, with discussion of quotes

. . . and so on.

Before you start, remember that in an examination most of the marks will probably be given for the detail with which you write about the text and for the way you explore quotations. Reviewing a text means going over the text in detail in your answer, analysing a text means identifying all the different aspects of a text that help you answer your question and commenting on a text is about exploring ideas in a text, often by writing about quotations. However, this unit is not just about what you say in your answer, it is also about how you write about your ideas. The better you are able to communicate your understanding to the examiner, the better your grade or level will be.

In each paragraph keep to this structure. The words in italics are an example to help you.

- Introduce the paragraph with a **clear topic sentence**:
The writer gives a clear description of the setting so that we can see in our minds where the action is taking place.

- Write a sentence to **expand or explain the idea** in your topic sentence, or to focus in on a particular detail. Maybe include a **drop-in clause** to add detail:
He describes the garden, full of rubbish, to show us that this is a place where no-one goes.

- Next give a **quotation**. Before the quotation put a comma and surround the quotation with speech marks:
He says, 'Weeds, blackened and shabby, had grown up against the house, grasping the stone in their clinging embrace'.

- Now pick out a **word** in the quotation to **comment** on. This is where you explore your ideas in more detail. This is where you can write in **complex sentences**, using **subordinate clauses** to make detailed points clearly and precisely. Put subordinate clauses in the middle or at the end of the sentence:
The phrase 'clinging embrace', describing the weeds, makes them sound evil, like they want to strangle the life out of the house. They make the house and garden seem like a place where there is no life, only death and decay.

- Next pick out **another example** to write about. This will ensure that you are developing ideas fully. After explaining your idea, copy a quotation and write about it, maybe identifying a key word. Maybe try to start with a subordinate clause:
After writing about the weeds, he goes on to describe the windows.
Or you could start your sentence with a passive:
The windows are described as broken, with jagged glass like teeth. This makes the reader . . .
The active would be: *The writer describes the windows as . . .* Using the passive helps put the focus of the sentence on the topic being discussed, in this case, the windows.

● Maybe try and **link** an idea to an earlier point:
The broken windows create the image of a skull, which builds on the earlier picture of a place where there is no life.

The structure is:

- start with a clear **topic sentence** to explain the main idea for the whole paragraph
- **explain** your idea, or focus on one part of the idea
- find a **quotation** to back up your idea
- **comment** on the quotation, pick out a key word to explore in detail
- **explain** the next point, which develops the first idea
- find another **quotation** to back up your idea
- **comment** on the quotation, picking out a key word or phrase and linking the point to your earlier idea.

When you are writing, remember to **vary your sentences**.

Use a mixture of **simple** and **complex** sentences. Often it is good to use a simple sentence at the beginning of a paragraph. For example, *The writer describes the thoughts of the characters.* This makes it very clear to the reader what you are going to write about.

When you write in complex sentences, **vary** where you put the **subordinate clauses**. For example, *The writer uses interesting verbs to give us very clear pictures of exactly what is happening* could also be written as: *To give us very clear pictures of exactly what is happening, the writer uses interesting verbs.*

Remember to start some sentences with the **passive** to throw the focus of the sentence onto the main topic of the sentence.

Don't forget all your **commas** to separate clauses from each other.

Alternate writing about what the **writer** is doing and what the effect is on the **reader**. So start some sentences with *The writer . . .* and some with *We, as readers, feel . . .*

Think about how one **paragraph** leads to the next and link them in your writing. For example, if you have been writing about the description of the setting and you then begin to write about the description of the characters, you could begin your paragraph with something like: *As well as giving us description of the setting, the writer also gives us a lot of information about the characters.*

Revising your draft

When you've finished your draft, check your work.

If you can, find six colours and underline the following in your writing in different colours:

- a subordinate clause at the beginning or end of a sentence
- a drop-in clause
- a sentence using the passive voice
- a quotation
- a comment on a quotation
- a sentence which develops an idea or links it to another.

You may find some sentences are underlined more than once!

Now put a circle around:

- all your connectives
- any words or phrases from the lists to create the right style
- an -ing word at the beginning of a subordinate clause.

Now answer the following questions about your draft:

- Is it **clear** what you have said? Ask your partner to read your draft. Ask them to mark places where they aren't sure what you mean. Ask them to mark places where the sentences don't follow on clearly.
- Have you ended each sentence with a **full stop**? (Count the number of sentences you have written in each paragraph. Write the number in the margin. Then count the number of full stops. The numbers should be the same!)
- Do all your sentences **begin with a capital letter**? (Underline the first word of each sentence. Has it got a capital letter?)
- Have you used **capital letters for names**? (Underline each name in what you have written. Put a ring round the first letter. Is it a capital?)

And:

- Have you used a **single comma** to **mark off words and phrases** from the rest of the sentence? (For example, *suddenly, just then, . . .*)
- Have you separated some of your **subordinate and co-ordinate clauses** from main clauses with **commas**?
- Have you put **pairs of commas** around clauses or phrases dropped into the middle of a sentence?

And:

- Have you written about most parts of the text?
- Have you used **vocabulary** that creates a **formal style** appropriate to this kind of writing?

And:

- And have you used a **topic sentence** when you start a new paragraph? (Underline the topic sentence in each paragraph.)

- Have you **developed** the topic sentence in the rest of the paragraph?
- Have you **linked** one paragraph to the next when appropriate?
- Have you included **quotations**?
- Have you **explored** the ideas you get from the words or phrases you have quoted?
- Have you **developed** ideas with a second quotation?

And finally:
- Check your draft carefully for the **spelling patterns** you know you have trouble with. (Use your spelling list to remind you.)

After underlining and circling, and after looking carefully at these questions you will have a good idea about what you need to do to your text.

Now write the final draft of your review. Make sure that your handwriting and overall presentation are as neat as possible.

Think-writing

Do some think-writing about how well you think you have done. Are there things you are feeling more confident about? Are there some things you still feel unsure about or you think you need more practise at? Did you find it hard to use passives, or subordinate clauses in a variety of ways? Did you put in all the commas?

When you are ready, review your progress using the grids from pages 71 and 72. What features of writing have you improved at? The more improvements you have made, the closer you are to a sound Level 6⁺.

And you could try . . .

The skills you have been learning in this unit will be useful for much of the writing you do both at Key Stage 3 and for GCSE. To further develop your skills, try one of the following tasks.

For each of the tasks you will need to find a text or texts to analyse.

- Find an extract in a novel or autobiography where we are made to feel sorry for a character, or made to feel angry at what has happened to a character. Then answer this question:

  How does the author make us as readers feel sympathy for, or angry with, the character in . . . ?

To make notes to help you answer the question, use the bullet points you used earlier in this unit to gather ideas for your analysis.

- For a more challenging task, read a whole novel and then answer this question:

  How does the author develop our understanding of the character, . . . in the novel, . . . ?

To make notes to help you answer this question, you will need to find about five extracts in the novel where the character you are writing about is the main focus of the story. For each of these places make notes on the way the writer has described the character's:

  - physical look
  - personality
  - thoughts and feelings
  - behaviour
  - opinions and attitudes toward events or other characters.

Notice if the character has changed at all since the last extract.

Choose and copy about five quotations from each of the extracts you are using.

When you write your analysis, the easiest way to organise your ideas is to write about how the writer develops our understanding in the first extract, then move onto the next. Keep linking your ideas back to points you had made earlier in the essay.

- You can also write about non-fiction texts. Find an advertisement with a lot of text on it and answer this question:

  How does the advert for . . . attempt to persuade you to buy the product?

To help you make notes, look back at the unit entitled 'Writing to persuade, argue, advise' on pages 47–66. Remind yourself of the techniques used in persuasive writing and then write about how effectively the writer of the advertisement has used those techniques.

Whatever you write about remember that to get a Level 6⁺, you must write in great detail, exploring ideas carefully. To make sure you do that, keep to this structure:

- start with a clear **topic sentence** to explain the main idea for the whole paragraph
- **explain** your idea, or focus on one part of the idea
- find a **quotation** to back up your idea
- **comment** on the quotation, picking out a key word to explore in detail
- **explain** the next point, which develops the first idea
- find another **quotation** to back up your idea
- **comment** on the quotation, picking out a key word or phrase and linking the point to your earlier idea.

When you are writing, remember to **vary your sentences**:

- use a mixture of **simple** and **complex** sentences
- when you write in complex sentences, **vary** where you put the **subordinate clauses**
- remember to start some sentences with the **passive** to throw the focus of the sentence onto the main topic of the sentence
- don't forget all your **commas** to separate clauses from each other
- **alternate** writing about what the **writer** is doing and what the effect is on the **reader**
- think about how one **paragraph** leads to the next and link them in your writing.

Remember you are:

Reviewing: going over the whole of the text, or extract of the text, so that the reader understands in detail what the text is about.

Analysing: exploring in detail your ideas about each part of the text and the text overall, using quotations as a launch pad to develop your ideas.

Commenting: giving your opinions about what the writer is saying and about how effectively he or she is saying it.